I AM NOT MY DRESS

VERA BROWN-SISLER

AUTHOR:
Vera Brown-Sisler
5198 Arlington Ave.
P.O. Box 273
Riverside, CA 92504-2603

www.verabrownsisler.com

All rights reserved. This book or any portion thereof may not be reproduced or used in any manner whatsoever without the express written permission of the author except for the use of brief quotations in a book review.

Unless otherwise indicated, Bible quotations are taken from The King James Version or paraphrased by the author.

Printed in the United States of America

PUBLISHER:
BUT GOD! Publishing
14910 Perris Blvd., Suite 126
Moreno Valley, CA 92553
EMAIL: butgodpublishings@gmail.com

Copyright © 2017 Vera Brown-Sisler
All rights reserved.
ISBN: 978-0-692-88864-3

DEDICATION

I dedicate this book to my husband, Ron, who (next to the Lord) is my most cherished friend. You are truly my Babio´ and a mighty man of valor. Thank you so very much for the support you have shown me over the years, and your unselfish love. I am your wife for life.

A special thanks to Terence Prosser for his talents and support in the proofreading of this book. You labored with me on this project, and I look forward to our next endeavor.

Most importantly, my sincere gratitude, to our Father in Heaven for His love, mercy, grace, and kindness. To God be all the honor, all the praise, and all the glory.

CONTENTS

	Dedication	Pg. 3
	Introduction	Pg. 5
1	Don't Judge the Book by Its Cover	Pg. 7
2	Stinking Thinking	Pg. 11
3	A New Way of Thinking	Pg. 15
4	Lips, Hips, and Fingertips	Pg. 19
5	Owning Your Power	Pg. 24
6	It's About Him	Pg. 33
7	I Almost Gave Up	Pg. 38
8	Find Your Why So You Can Fly	Pg. 44
9	A Date with Destiny	Pg. 49
10	Find Opportunity in Rejection	Pg. 59
11	Determined to Keep on Going	Pg. 68
12	Your Best Is Within Reach	Pg. 75
13	In the Face of Fear	Pg. 81
14	It's an Inside Job	Pg. 98
15	Dismiss Distractions	Pg. 105
16	From This Day Forward	Pg. 113
17	The Dress Looks Good on You	Pg. 124
18	Everyone is Unique	Pg. 128

INTRODUCTION

Vera noticed that her workout clothes hugged her waist, and her wrapped dresses showed off her curves. She is a curvy woman; thus, the protrusions of her anatomy are not uncommon. Her sister and nieces bring to light a flattering remark about her hourglass figure. Like Vera, many African-American women have been dubbed "Brick House" or "36-24-36." Vera likes to wear vibrant colors. She loves all the lively shades. Bright colors are her forte, and the more the merrier. However, she is still confused as to why judgments are made based upon the cloth on ones back.

Vera's clothes, which dance in the wind, do not represent who she is. When she looks down at her body, she sees clothes as a piece of artwork. Do not formulate opinions of her based on clothing. Do not measure her worth based on the color of the dress. What she knows for sure is that she has a purpose to fulfill and a legacy to leave. She is a curvy woman and a woman of many colors, but Vera is *not* just her dress.

This book has been like an unborn child, and the pregnancy has gone too far past full term. If this child is not born, it will cause great discomfort to the one carrying it. The nursery is painted, the mobiles are hanging over the crib, and dozens of onesies are perfectly folded in a dresser drawer. The anticipation of giving birth is as a fire shut up in your bones. So, where's the baby? The book you hold in your hands is that baby; it is a noteworthy conversation piece for all women who are looked at as mannequins in a dress at a retail store.

In the pages that follow, you will find insight, self-confidence and a declaration of independence as I share stories of beliefs, convictions, dreams, and yes struggles from my own life. The door is wide open for you to realize your dreams, walk confidently into your future, and never look back. Fear, setbacks, rejection, and disappointments cannot abort the determination in you. Let's get started!

CHAPTER 1
Don't Judge the Book by Its Cover

*Therefore if any man be in Christ, he is a
new creature: old things are passed away;
behold, all things are become new.*
2 Corinthians 5:17

Boiled okra is one of those vegetables that you either love or hate. It never appealed to me due to its slimy exterior; however, as not to offend my mother-in-law, I tried it. To my surprise, it was good. I quickly learned that you should not judge a book by its cover. Yet, like it or not, every day we are judged by our outside appearance. Too often, we see what is on the outside as being the total package. I am sick of it!

Real beauty is not in a dress. Beauty is in the soul. It is a kindness given, thoughtfulness shared, goodness bestowed – these things will long be remembered. The wise do not buy into others' perception of who they are and what they are capable of doing. Instead, they bypass the court of public opinion and see that they are the light of the world. "A city set on a hill cannot be hidden" (Matthew 5:14). Don't judge the book by its cover. It's what's inside that counts!

We have a difficult time looking past the outer shell. We bypass the inner robe of righteousness and overlook the Fruits of the Spirit that lay on the inside. For example, in order to bake a cake from scratch you must start with the ingredients (what goes inside of the cake). Those ingredients include: flour, baking powder, eggs, milk, vegetable oil or butter, and usually some flavoring such as vanilla extract. Then you smother in the frosting. In the same way, a person should not focus their attention on the exterior but the interior instead. It is interesting that God never called attention to the exterior. Although Mary wrapped baby Jesus in swaddling clothes and laid Him in a manger, don't let the clothes fool you. Jesus' swaddling clothes were part of the "sign" to the shepherds of His identity as the Savior (Luke 2:12). We had better start concerning ourselves with what Jesus is concerned with: the heart, the inner man and the spirit within. This reference is not about the heart as a vital organ (a muscle that pumps blood through the body), neither is it in regards to romantic, philosophical, or storybook definitions. What follows, are examples from the Bible of how to direct your heart to follow hard after God, and judge things God's way.

The Bible mentions the human heart almost 300 times. In essence, this is what it says: the heart is the spiritual part of us where our emotions and desires dwell. We have a heart because God has a heart. "David was a man after God's own heart" (Acts 13:22). David, a sheepherder, was the son of Jesse of Bethlehem. He was anointed by Samuel to be successor to King Saul who was the first king of the united Israel. God blesses His people with leaders who know and follow His heart (1 Samuel 2:35; Jeremiah 3:15).

The heart is the core of our being, and the Bible sets high importance on keeping our hearts pure. "Above all else, guard your heart, for it is the wellspring of life" (Proverbs 4:23). We live in a very superficial society where it is easy to fall into the trap of looking at the surface (for instance: clothing, shoes, and material possessions) without taking the time and effort to delve deeper. This is where the adage, "Don't Judge a Book by Its Cover" comes from. Literally, you cannot tell the quality of a book's contents just by looking at the material used to hold it together. That is because it's not what's on the outside that matters; it's what's on the inside.

DECLARATION OF OWNERSHIP (I)

THE POWER OF I AM
Thou shall also decree a thing, and it shall be established unto thee: and the light shall shine upon thy ways.
Job 22:28

I AM A WOMAN OF INTEGRITY
A good name is rather to be chosen than great riches, and loving favour rather than silver and gold.
Proverbs 22:1

I AM A WOMAN OF CHARACTER
Withhold no good from them to whom it is due, when it is in the power of thine hand to do it.
Proverbs 3:27

I AM A WOMAN OF MY WORD
*I have more understanding than all my teachers: for thy testimonies are my meditation.
I understand more than the ancients because I keep thy precepts.*
Psalm 119:99-100

I AM A WOMAN OF EXCELLENCE
He that hath knowledge spareth his words: a man of understanding is of an excellent spirit.
Proverbs 17:27

I AM A LEADING LADY
Thou therefore, my son, be strong in the grace that is in Christ Jesus. And the things thou hast heard of me among many witnesses, the same commit thou to faithful men, who shall be able to teach others also.
2 Timothy 2:1-2

I AM HOLY
Because it is written: Be ye holy, for I am holy.
1 Peter 15:16

CHAPTER 2
Stinking Thinking

For I know the thoughts that I think toward you, saith the Lord, thoughts of peace, and not of evil, to give you an expected end.
Jeremiah 29:11

Negative thinking is primarily a state of mind that influences a person to look at things with a pessimistic attitude instead of an optimistic attitude. Negativity is a menacing evil that is both depressing and disgusting; having the ability to ruin relationships, destroy health and cause depression. Some people are walking around with a medicine chest in their pockets, as studies have determined that more people are on prescribed anti-depressants today than yesterday. Most people tend to cover up their feelings of negativity and depression with alcohol, drugs, and pills instead of finding out the root cause and eradicating it.

The way to stop this "stinking thinking" is to simply start thinking positively. Yet, as simple as that sounds, it is not always easy. If you really want to get out of the rut of "stinking thinking" and do better things, you must lay aside every heavy burden that encourages negative thinking.

Being hyper fault-finding of my own appearance is something I've struggled with significantly at times in my life. Some of the deepest pain and self-loathing I've ever felt has been connected to me feeling ugly and not good enough physically. I am sure that there are a variety of external factors that have contributed to some degree as well. For example, growing up with parents who did not feel good about themselves mentally and physically did not help my personal development skills; however, at the root of my issues is a deep sense of feeling fundamentally flawed – mentally and emotionally.

My elementary school experience was comprised of unsympathetic teachers and unending bullies. Bullying is a big problem. It can make kids feel hurt, scared, sick, lonely, embarrassed, sad, and fearful. The National Education Association estimated that 160,000 children miss school every day due to fear of attack or intimidation by other students. Those in lower grades reported being in twice as many fights as those in higher grades. However, there is a lower rate of serious violent crimes on the elementary level versus the middle or high school levels. It can be hard for adults, including parents, to know whether a child is being bullied. A child might not tell anyone because they're scared the bullying will get worse. They might think that they deserve to be bullied or that it's their fault. That means we have to do everything we can to understand bullying and find the best ways to keep children safe. You can't always see the signs of bullying; and, no one sign indicates that a child is being bullied. But, the following might be clues:

Bullying and Cyber Bullying: Signs, Symptoms, and Effects

Bullying is a repeated verbal, physical, social or psychological behavior that is harmful and involves the misuse of power by an individual(s).

- *Come home with torn, damaged, or missing pieces of clothing*

- *Have unexplained cuts, bruises, and scratches from fighting*

- *Seem afraid of going to school or walking to and from school*

- *Lose interest in schoolwork or suddenly begin to do poorly in school*

- *Appear sad, moody, teary, or depressed when she or he comes home*

- Dr. Dan Olweus, Research Professor of Psychology
 Source: Olweus Bulling Prevention Program

DECLARATION OF OWNERSHIP (II)

THE POWER OF I AM
For as a man thinketh in his heart, so is he.
Proverbs 23:7

I AM ANOINTED
Touch not mine anointed, and do my prophets no harm.
Psalm 105:15

I AM CREATIVE
*I have shewed thee new things from this time,
even hidden things, and thou didst not know them.*
Isaiah 48:6

I AM BLAMELESS
*For he hath made him to be sin for us, who knew no sin;
that we might be made the righteous of God in him.*
2 Corinthians 5:21

I AM DETERMINED
If thou faint in the day of adversity, thy strength is small.
Proverbs 24:10

I AM MOTIVATED
*Be strong and of good courage, fear not, nor be afraid of
them: for the Lord thy God, He is that doth go with thee; He
will not fail thee, nor forsake thee.*
Deuteronomy 31:6

I AM GIFTED
*A man's gift maketh room for him,
and bringeth him before great men.*
Proverbs 18:16

I AM TALENTED
*Every good and perfect gift is from above,
and cometh down from the Father of lights,
With whom is no variableness, neither shadow of turning.*
James 1:17

CHAPTER 3
A New Way of Thinking

*And have put on the new man, which is renewed
in knowledge after the image of Him that created him.*
Colossians 3:10

A new way of thinking means to change your thoughts. Change is the key word, and we see it happening everywhere. The seasons change from summer to fall, to winter, and to spring. As a matter of fact, Ecclesiastes 3:1 says that there is a time for everything and a season. A positive change should bring about a new way of thinking. We need to recognize change as a paradigm shift: new ideas to replace the traditional ones. Remember, the journey of a thousand miles begins with a single step. You simply have to take the first one.

Change is the only constant in life. All species must evolve or die. When we change, we grow. We evolve physically, mentally, emotionally, and spiritually. Infants are not born adults. There are three stages of development from a newborn baby into an adult. There are also some developmental milestones such as motor, speech, vision, hearing, and social skills. Boys become men, and girls become women. We have a body, a soul, and a spirit. We develop thinking skills; some learned, some taught, and some discovered. We are shaped by our thoughts. We become what we think (Proverbs 23:7). When the mind is clear, it follows like a shadow that never leaves. If you realize how powerful your thoughts are, you may never speak another negative word again. Believe that you are worthy of your heart's desires. Make meaningful thoughts count, and give birth to those thoughts. Find a way to tap into the resources that will assist you in becoming all you want to be.

We all want a progressive lifestyle, but if there's no direction, no discipline, and no determination then we are easy prey for the devil, and we will fail every time. The devil's main goals are to get you off course, out of the will of God, and to trick you out of your inheritance. I am reminded of the Bible narrative of twin brothers Esau and Jacob, the sons of Isaac and Rebekah and the first twins mentioned in the Bible. Even before they were born, they were struggling together in the womb of their mother. Their prenatal striving foreshadowed later friction (Genesis 25:27-34).

The twins grew up very differently. Jacob was "a quiet man, staying near home" and his mother's favorite. Esau was "a skillful hunter, an outdoorsman" and his father's favorite (Genesis 25:27). One day, Esau returned from hunting hungry, and desired some of the boiled pottage that Jacob was cooking. Jacob offered to give his brother some lentil stew in exchange of his birthright – the special honor that Esau possessed as the older son, which gave him the right to a double portion of his father's inheritance. Due to Esau's lack of willpower, he gave away his God-given blessing and sold his birthright.

When the time came for Isaac to bestow his blessings upon his sons, Jacob and his mother plotted to deceive Isaac into blessing Jacob instead of Esau. When Esau found that his blessing had been given to Jacob, he threatened to kill his brother, and Jacob fled (Genesis 27:1-45). Years later, Jacob and Esau met and were reconciled (Genesis 33).

A new way of thinking is being responsible for your own life and being accountable for the decisions you've made. We have the ability to change our lives for the better. With each choice comes a consequence, and no amount of rationalizing will alter that consequence. "Do not be deceived God is not mocked; whatever a man soweth that he will also reap" (Galatians 6:7). You can take control of your life; be a victor not a victim. What choices are you making today?

DECLARATION OF OWNERSHP (PART III)

THE POWER OF I AM
Therefore, if anyone is in Christ, he is a new creation; old things have passed away; and behold, all things have become new.
2 Corinthians 5:17

I AM MORE THAN A CONQUEROR
Nay, in all these things I am more than a Conqueror through him that loved us.
Romans 8:37

I AM A FAITH WALKER
Now faith is the substance of things hoped for, and the evidence of things not seen.
Hebrews 11:1

I AM HIGHLY FAVORED OF THE LORD
And the angel came unto her, and said hail, thou that art highly favoured, the Lord is with thee: blessed art thou among women.
Luke 1:28

I AM A PROVERBS 31 WOMAN
Who can find a virtuous woman? For her price is far above rubies. The heart of her husband doth safely trust her, so that he shall have no need of spoil. She will do him good and not evil all the days of her life.
Proverbs 31:10-12

She seeketh wool, and flax, and worketh willingly with her hands.
Proverbs 31:14

I AM CREATIVE
Trust in the Lord with all thine heart; and lean not unto thine own understanding. In all thy ways acknowledge him, and he shall direct thy paths.
Proverbs 3:5-6

CHAPTER 4
Lips, Hips, and Fingertips

*Having therefore these promises, dearly beloved,
let us cleanse ourselves from all filthiness of the
flesh and spirit, perfecting holiness in the fear of God.
2 Corinthians 7:1*

Several years ago, there was a documentary on TV about a farmer whose geese hatched eggs. Upon hatching, he was the first thing the chicks saw, so they thought he was their mother. They followed him everywhere. When winter approached, these geese were supposed to fly south. However, they wouldn't go without him. So, he did something unusual. He got himself a small airplane and guided them south. He flew right beside them and got them safely to the southern part of the states. But, if he had not guided them south in that little plane, they would never have gone. Just like the farmer, Christians must be imitators of God; mirroring His love, kindness, compassion, and forgiveness.

Ephesians 5:1 says, "Be ye imitators of God." We are called to be like God. We are called to be holy. Colossians 1:27 reminds us that people should see Christ in us. When they look at us, they are to see nothing less than the attributes of God! We are to show them what God is like. One mistake we make in regards to holiness is that we sometimes act as if other human beings are the standard of holiness; but, only God is the model for holiness.

God is unlike any other. His holiness is perfect. On the other hand, man is imperfect and subject to fail. Matthew 5:48 says, "Be ye therefore perfect, even as your Father which is in heaven is perfect." Jesus urges us to exhibit characteristics like God. Roman 8:29 instructs us to conform to the likeness of His Son. But just what does it mean to be holy (set apart)? We see this in Genesis 2:3, "Then God blessed the seventh day and sanctified it. He rested from all his work, which he created and made." If we want to feel beautiful, we need to start by changing the way we think about beauty.

It's not just about the lips, hips, and fingertips that sometimes shape your life. I want to remind you that you are beautiful in your own skin. God's definition of beauty is that you're fearfully and wonderfully made. He knew exactly what He was doing when He created you. Whether you are tall or short, slim or shapely; whether your skin tone is light or dark, and your hair is long or short, the Lord looks at your heart. Proverbs 4:23 says, "Keep thy heart with all diligence; for out of it are the issues of life."

I must admit, when I first joined the gym my motivation was to look good. I mean, to look very good. I wanted my body to be ripped, lean, toned, slim, and curvy. I had, and still have, a false perception that if I go to the gym five days a week I can have my cake and eat it too. And, although diet and exercise are vital for long-term weight loss, you aren't really going to see the results you're hoping for unless you find a blueprint that puts all the necessary factors in place. "For bodily exercise, you will profit little; but, godliness is profitable. Physical training is of some value, but godliness has value for all things" (1 Timothy 4:8).

As Christians, we are not to value the things the world values. One of the significant callings that God puts in the hearts of Christians is the call to be holy. Holiness starts in the mind and requires personal discipline. Personal discipline causes you to do things that should be done. How else will we get things done? How else will we achieve holiness? The Apostle Paul acknowledged in Romans 7:19, "For the good that I would I do not: but the evil, which I would not, that I do." Our words and deeds must be pleasing to God. Believers in Jesus Christ are simply in the world – physically present, but not of it; not a part of its values. Holiness has no shelf life. Holiness is not a sprint. Holiness is a marathon, a continuous body in motion. The Christian life is a difficult marathon that we must run with all diligence.

Many years ago, a young woman who was addicted to drugs professed that she believed in Christ. She was a single parent with two small children. On one occasion, when she was relatively sober of excessive alcohol consumption, I described in detail to her what a daily walk with Christ looks like. I explained what a daily time in the Bible and prayer is like, what obedience to the Word of God means, and how to think like a Christian. When I was done, I asked, "Have you ever done anything close to what I've just described?" She said, "Yeah, I did that once for two weeks, but it didn't work." She thought that she had given it a fair try in two weeks! I explained to her that the Christian faith isn't a two-week sprint. It's a lifelong marathon.

The Christian life entails some long hills to climb, mountains to scale, valleys to plod, disappointments to endure, sleepless nights, and sickness and diseases to fight against. But, when you have done all you can, let God into your heart and He will give you peace that passes all understanding.

The remainder of this book will deal with the champion in you and the necessary action steps to propel you forward in spite of opposition or difficulties.

DECLARATION OF OWNERSHIP (III)

THE POWER OF I AM
*For I say, through the grace given unto me,
to every man that is among you,
not to think of himself more highly than he ought to think;
but to think soberly according as God hath dealt to every
man the measure of faith.*
Romans 12:3

I AM SPECIAL
Behold, I have graven thee upon the palms of my hands.
Isaiah 49:16

I AM VALUABLE
*I have made a covenant with my chosen,
I have sworn unto David my servant,
my covenant will I not break, nor alter the thing that is gone
out of My lips.*
Psalm 89:3-4

I AM BEAUTIFUL
*I will praise thee; I am fearfully and wonderfully made:
marvelous are thy works; and that my soul knoweth right
well.*
Psalm 139:14

I AM FORGIVEN
*If we confess our sins,
he is faithful and just to forgive us our sins,
and to cleanse us from all unrighteousness.*
1 John 1:9

I AM A JEWEL
*He that dwelleth in the secret place of the Most High shall
abide under the shadow of the almighty. I will say of the
Lord, He is my refuge and my fortress: my God; in him will
I trust. Surely he shall deliver thee from the snare of the
fowler, and from the noisome pestilence.*
Psalm 91:1-3

CHAPTER 5
Owning Your Power

*Behold I give unto you power to tread on serpents
and scorpions, and all the power of the enemy
and nothing shall by any means hurt you.*
Luke 10:19

When you own something, it is paid for in full. That is the way it is with life. There is no layaway or payment plan because Jesus paid it all some two thousand years ago. On the cross, the Lord Jesus Christ shed His precious blood to pay for our sins. When we repent of our sins and believe in the death, burial and resurrection of Jesus Christ, then we are saved by grace (Ephesians 2:8).

Maybe you don't feel like you have power because you have experienced some setbacks, roadblocks, and potholes in your life. But, the Bible says, "Behold, I have given you power to tread on serpents and scorpions, and all the power of the enemy: and "NOTHING" shall by any means hurt you" (Luke 10:19). You are a child of "The Most High God." All power has been given to you on Earth (and under Earth). When there is a head-on collision between the power of the enemy and the power of God, the power of the enemy will lose every time. Jesus's power is greater than that of the enemy. So, how then do we live and walk in this power and authority?

The pathway to greatness occurs when you shift your focus from success to servanthood. It was once said that, "The two greatest days of your life are the day you were born and the day you find out what your purpose is." It is important for you to search your inner soul to identify your purpose for it is the very reason you exist. Anything in life is possible and you can make it happen. Greatness isn't reserved for a preordained few. It is available to you and me. Greatness ignites the fire, but purpose keeps the fire blazing.

Here's an inspiring story about Jack LaLanne that I read on his website. Jack was a motivational speaker and an American fitness, exercise, and nutritional expert who set the stage for owning his purpose through exercise. Throughout his seventy-plus year career, he motivated millions throughout the world to help themselves by improving their health through simple goals, challenges and a healthy lifestyle. Not only did Jack LaLanne have the first modern health studio, which opened in 1936, but he was also a pioneer in television. He was known as the man that started the fitness revolution and he is often called "The Godfather of Fitness." He commonly said, "Exercise is King, Nutrition is Queen, put them together and you have a Kingdom." As a member of God's kingdom, you don't have to settle for a meaningless life.

While there are many ways to discover your purpose in life, here's one of the simplest: Rid yourself of the thought that it will fall out of the sky. You have your purpose within you. Nicolas Sparks, writer and novelist, believes that, "Too many people live their lives acting, pretending, wearing masks, and losing themselves in the process." God wants us to take our masks off and reveal the genuine beauty of our true selves.

I am a country girl born on a farm in Lamar, Mississippi. I am one of those girls that you can take out of the country, but you can't take the country out of the girl. We had several farm animals: cows, horses, hogs, and chickens. Chickens are fearful. Most of the time, chickens hang together in a pack; if one ran, they all ran. When there's rain, storm, thunder, or lightening, chickens run and hide.

Chickens can barely lift themselves off of the ground. Unlike a chicken, an eagle flies high. Chickens run away from the storm, but the eagle flies into the storm. The book of Isaiah (in the Old Testament section of the Bible) makes us the promise, "Those who wait on the Lord shall renew their strength; they shall mount up with wings of eagles; they shall run, and not be weary; they shall walk, and not faint" (Isaiah 40:31). Storms are inevitable. If you are not in a storm, you just got out of one and are on your way back into another one. You must be storm proof. You must look at your storm through the eyes of the Lord and declare, "Nay in all these things I am more than a conqueror" (Romans 8:28). The best day of your life is the one on which you decide to own your power.

In 1973, I moved from Memphis, Tennessee (population over one million) to Los Angeles, California (population over three million). Needless to say, I experienced significant culture shock. I was a country girl, not a city girl. I had never seen a McDonald's, never eaten Mexican food, and never seen a Hispanic person. In Memphis, it rained almost every day. In California, it was sunny almost every day.

In January 2015, Governor Jerry Brown declared a State of Emergency and directed state officials to take all necessary actions to prepare for the water shortages. Grappling with drought conditions, California officials approved statewide emergency water restrictions. Those restrictions affected car washing between the hours of 6:00 p.m. and 6:00 a.m. Infractions brought fines of five hundred dollars per day. Some water agencies offered homeowners rebates to replace their yard with drought tolerant landscapes. Farmers in pockets of California hardest hit by the drought could begin to see their wells run dry if rain and snow remained scarce.

In the natural, we see water all around us. We drink it for survival. We bathe in it. We wash with it. When it doesn't rain, we pray deeply for it. Two of my favorite places to visit are San Francisco and San Diego to see the beautiful oceans with streams of water. The Bible has a lot to say about water.

The first time water was mentioned in the Bible was in the Old Testament. In Genesis 1:2, it says, "The earth was without form, and void; and darkness was on the face of the deep. And the Spirit of God was hovering over the face of the waters." From Genesis to Revelation, water flows throughout the Holy Scriptures. These narratives and scriptures connect water to God's love, forgiveness and salvation for His people. The Bible narrative of "The Woman at the Well" evidences this.

John 4:3-4 says, "Jesus and His disciples left Judea and departed again to Galilee. But He needed to go through Samaria." Much like today, the mixed multitudes of Samaritans were not accepted by the Jewish people because of their bitter history. Although the Jews did not like the Samaritans, Jesus purposefully went through their territory.

In Samaria, Jesus arrived at a place called Jacob's Well. He was tired, hot, and needed rest from the long travel by foot. Jesus sent His disciples to find some food. While they were gone, Jesus met the Samaritan woman at the well. He asked her for a drink of water. We don't know her name, age, skill set, or how many children she had; but, what we do know is that she was a Samaritan, she had five husbands, and the man she was currently "shacking up" with was not her husband.

Jesus never condemned her. He looked at her kindly and explained, "He who drinks of this water will never thirst again." His one-on-one conversation about grace prompted her to run and tell everybody who would listen that Jesus had taken a life that was drifting and given it direction and purpose. Instead of giving her power and virtue away now she could own her power.

What I've learned from "The Woman at the Well" is not to seek men for validation. Listen, if you don't get anything else from this chapter you must absolutely know without a shadow of a doubt *who you are in Christ!* Jesus Christ has set the standard in His Word. Psalm 139:14 says that you are fearfully and wonderfully made. That means that God doesn't make any unwanted items. Everything He makes is good.

Your journey is based on owning your power. But, often you cannot do that because you have not truthfully let go of the wounds of the past. Another reason is often negative thinking. You are your own worst critic. Say, "Amen!" You're always putting yourself down or you're letting the devil put you down. The devil is supposed to be under your foot. Why is he in your ear? Why is the devil in front of you when he is supposed to be behind you?

By submitting to the Word of God, you have the ability to resist the devil and he will flee. The Word of God is sharper than a double-edged sword; it cuts going and coming. If you want to own your power then stop accepting what other people think about you. It's what you think about you that matters the most. Consider the saying, "If it's going to be it's up to me." Proverbs 4:23 says, "Keep your heart with all diligence for out of it springs the issues of life."

Harness your own power because people can be hard taskmasters. Hard taskmasters are always putting themselves first. They're always pushing their agenda and their purpose without considering that you have an agenda and a purpose as well. How do you learn how to own your power? You practice The Principle of Replacement. This means that you trade in negative thoughts for positive thoughts. "Do not be conformed to this world, but be transformed by the renewing of your mind, that you may prove what is that good and acceptable and perfect will of God" (Romans 12:2). You will never own your power with yesterday's negative thoughts.

Change the way you think or become what you think. For instance, if you think failure then you are a failure. If you think success then you are a success. You must see yourself there before you get there. It's not about what happened to you, it's about what you are going to do about it. You have power working in you just because you woke up this morning. Say, "It's in me!" Talk to yourself. Here are five tidbits that will jumpstart and catapult you into owning your power:

Number one. *Don't be afraid to put yourself first.* If you don't help yourself then you can't help anyone else (and all the praying in the world won't help either). As an adult, when you are traveling by air with a child, the airline attendant tells you during the safety demonstration that in case of an emergency landing you must put your life jacket on first. Make yourself a priority.

Number two. *Don't apologize for being blessed and favored by God.* Your testimony is not for you. Your testimony is used to tell others that if God blessed you, He will do it for them too. I often say that God is not a respecter of persons but a respecter of faith. The only person you are to apologize to is yourself for not telling others about how big your God is. 3 John 2 says, "Beloved I wish above all things that thou mayest prosper and be in health, even as your soul prospereth." Not only that but Revelation 12:11a says, "They overcame him by the blood of the Lamb, and by the word of their testimony.

Number three. *Don't feel guilty about being blessed by God.* If God is in the blessing business (and He is) that means you are next in line. Why should you feel guilty? You are a servant of Jesus Christ. You carry the seed of Isaac, Abraham and Jacob. You are an heir to all His promises. "The promises of God are yea and amen and they add no sorrow" (2 Corinthians 1:20).

Number four. *Don't limit your thinking.* Think big. We serve a God that has been tested in the fire, the storm, and the drought. No matter what the problem is, God is bigger than any of your wants or needs, and stronger than your toughest problem. And what's so wonderful about Him is that, "He is the same yesterday, today, and forever" (Hebrews 13:8). God is not double-minded. He does not have Dementia or Alzheimer's. He knows His thoughts and plans towards you. He knows you inside and out, and all the ugly mess in between. God is faithful. He will not let you down. You can count on God to come through for you. When you have a history with God, you can go way back and draw on your empty bank account. And because He loves you, He will open the storehouse to fill and refill your empty jars and barrels.

God has given us the power to speak things into existence. All you need to do is own that power. The second you do that, the old things will pass away and all things will become new. You will receive a new mindset, a new attitude and radical power that you never realized you had. When people reject you, marginalize you, devalue and criticize you, keep in mind that you are not defeated by what they say or do, you are defeated if you believe what they say about you. Some people are waiting for your downfall. Use your power to prove them wrong.

The only way to have power is you must own it. Never underestimate the power of passion. The enemy will make you feel unequipped, empty, and unfit, but it is imperative that you speak God's Word over your life. God will watch over His Word to perform it (Jeremiah 1:12). His Word will not return void. Don't settle for manufactured power. Only accept the tangible power that you can reach out and touch. Awaken your best self and own your power. Stop wishing and start doing. Every day is a new day to command. Commanding your life will liberate your inner awesomeness.

DECLARATION OF OWNERSHIP (IV)

THE POWER OF I AM
*And the Lord answered me, and said,
Write the vision, and make it plain upon the tablets, that he may run that readeth it.*
Habakkuk 2:2

I AM PREGNANT WITH DESTINY
For the vision is yet for an appointed time, but at the end it shall speak, and not lie: though it tarry, wait for it, because it will surely come. it will not tarry. Behold, his soul which is lifted is not upright in him: but the just shall live by faith.
Habakkuk 2:2-3

I AM NOT A QUITTER
Casting all your cares upon him; for he careth for you.
1 Peter 5:7

I AM A WINNER
Fear thou not; for I am with thee: be not dismayed for I am thy God: I will strengthen thee; yea, I will help thee, I will uphold thee with the right hand of my righteousness
Isaiah 41:10

I AM CHRIST-LIKE
But the fruit of the Spirit is love, joy, peace, longsuffering, gentleness, goodness, and faith
Galatians 5:22

I AM THE RIGHTEOUSNESS OF GOD
*I have been young, and now I am old;
yet have I not seen the righteousness forsaken,
nor His seed begging bread*
Psalm 37:25

CHAPTER 6
It's About Him

That I might know him, and the power of his resurrection, and the fellowship of his sufferings, being made conformable unto his death.
Philippians 3:10

Are we thinking like man or are we thinking like God? It's great to know that God doesn't think like us. "For my thoughts are not your thoughts, neither are your ways my ways, saith the Lord. For as the heavens are higher than the earth, so are my ways higher than your ways, and my thoughts than your thoughts" (Isaiah 55:8-9).

In what ways is Jesus higher than I? First, God is all-powerful. "In the beginning was the Word, and the Word was with God, and the Word was God" (John 1:1). He has always existed. We must remember that, "The secret things belong unto the Lord our God: but those things which are revealed belong to us and to our children forever" (Deuteronomy 29:29). He created the heavens and the Earth. He lifted the sun, stars, and the moon. He fashioned mountains into existence. He measured the waters. He made everything. There is no limit to His power.

Second, God is omniscient. He is all-knowing. He knows the innermost thoughts of our hearts, and He even knows what we are going to say before we say it. He knows us from the top of our heads to the soles of our feet. He knows everything about us; the good, the bad, and the ugly. God knows everything, including what's going to happen in the future. He is the Alpha and Omega, the beginning and the end, the first and the last (Revelation 22:13).

Third, God is omnipresent. He is present in every place throughout the universe. He is not limited by space. The Psalmist wrote: "Where can I go from your spirit? Or where can I flee from your presence? If I ascend into heaven, you are there; if I take the wings of the morning and dwell in the uttermost parts of the sea, even there your hand shall lead me, and your right hand shall hold me. If I say, 'Surely the darkness will hide me, and the light become night around me,' even the darkness will not be dark to you; the night will shine like the day, for the darkness is as light to you" (Psalm 139:7-12). God is everywhere at once.

When I was a young woman, I continually wrestled with knowing God's will for my life. I still wrestle with doing His will in my life. Staying in the center of His plan is a lifelong pursuit. So, how can we know God's plan for our lives? Over the past 20 years that I have been in ministry, I have discovered that you must know Him first. You need to develop a relationship with Him. That is His desire. Christianity is all about relationship rather than religion.

Furthermore, you must cultivate your relationship with God. You must seek to know Him, not just seek to know about Him. How do you get to know a person? You must spend some time with them. You will cultivate that relationship best by spending time in His Word, taking time for prayer, and taking every opportunity you can to be involved in church and small group Bible studies. When you seek these disciplines in your life, God will begin the first steps to revealing His plan to you.

Many times when we say we are seeking God's will, we are telling Him, "Here's my plan. Lord, will you sign, seal, and deliver it?" But, you cannot manipulate

God. His ways and thoughts are not our ways and thoughts. God knows the plans He has for you (Jeremiah 29:11). All you need to do is follow the plan (His plans that will always be related to the gifts He has graciously given to you) and be confident that you will be great at doing His will. Learn to be patient and know that your gift will make room for you (Proverbs 18:16).

DECLARATION OF OWNERSHIP (V)

THE POWER OF I AM
*For God so loved the world, that
he gave His only begotten Son, that
whosoever believeth in Him should
not perish, but have everlasting life.*
John 3:16

I AM GOD'S WORKMANSHIP
*For the perfecting of the saints, for the work of the ministry,
for the edifying of the body of* Christ.
Ephesians 4:12

I AM THE LIGHT OF THE WORLD
*In the beginning God created the heavens and the earth.
And the earth was without form, and void; and darkness
was upon the face of the deep. And the Spirit of God moved
upon the face of the waters.
And God said, "Let there be light," and there was light.*
Genesis 1:1-3

I AM A CHILD OF GOD
*But as many received him, to him gave he power
to become the sons of God,
even to them that believe on his name.*
John 1:12

I AM A FRIEND OF JESUS
*Henceforth I call you not servants;
for the servant knoweth not what his lord doeth:
but I have called you friends;
for all things that I have heard of my Father I have made
known unto you.*
John 15:15

I AM ONE SPIRIT WITH THE LORD
But he that is joined unto the Lord is one spirit.
1 Corinthians 6:17

I AM A MEMBER OF CHRIST'S BODY
Now ye are the body of Christ, and member's in particular.
1 Corinthians 12:27

CHAPTER 7
I Almost Gave Up

*Weeping may endure for a night,
but joy cometh in the morning.
Psalm 30:5*

How many times have you decided in your mind that what you were doing was not working, and you were wasting your time? How many times have you felt like you were spinning your wheels? How many times have you felt stuck? Stuck but hopeful. Trapped but determined. I have been there. In the midst of being stuck and trapped, I felt a Godly nagging in my spirit proving to me that He was on my side; demonstrating His goodness, kindness, mercy, and grace. The Lord has been gracious, and blessed me with the necessities of life such as food, water, and shelter. We have the basic needs covered; however, we still have financial, familial, emotional, and health related needs.

Many of us are sick with various illnesses and diseases, walking around in excruciating pain, and just about to give up on life because of disorders, sickness, aches here, aches there, and aches everywhere. But, I don't believe God has brought us this far to abandon us. I just don't believe it. Keep on walking by faith and talking faith. One of the tactics the devil uses is to make you worry, and doubt God's infallible Word. The job of the enemy is to make the Word of God ineffective. You must be careful of his ways. The enemy will not get in your face and make you doubt all of the time; instead, most of the time, he is incredibly subtle, sly, and clever. The devil is likened unto a gardener. He plants seeds of doubt, discord, and disbelief. Then, he will let the doubt, discord, and disbelief simmer in your mind with a constant nagging.

After a period of time, he will come along and water those seeds with more doubt, more discord, and more disbelief in order to make you want to give up on being healed, delivered, and set free.

Jesus calls the enemy the "prince of this world, and the father of lies." The Bible calls him "the god of this world," who blinds the eyes and the ears of believers and unbelievers (2 Corinthians 4:4). Scriptures constantly warn the church against the wiles of the devil and his methods, using wording like: "be not deceived" and "be vigilant." Has the devil had any influence on you? Has the devil led you astray? God allows U-turns. In John 10:10, Jesus is depicted as "The Good Shepherd" who laid His life down for the sheep. The church is God's flock made of sheep that "The Good Shepherd" has rescued. The sheep know the shepherd's voice and obey it; they will not follow if they hear another voice. There are many voices calling us today, and some of them even sound holy. But the true children of God will not follow when they hear the voice of strangers. The Bible admonishes us to guard our gates so we won't go astray; but, here's the problem, we don't do a good enough job of guarding our eyes and ears. We let bad stuff come into our minds.

All of the hard work we put into building ourselves up with the Word of God and praying is compromised when we do not guard our eyes and ears. God-fearing Christians are falling by the wayside. They are giving up on God. You might be one of those people who are thinking about giving up. But, God has not brought you this far to leave you. He has not forgotten about you. I don't care how many people around you are being blessed. Be confident of this one thing, "God has begun a good work in you, and will perform it until the day of

Jesus Christ" (Philippians 1:6). You might not understand what's going on, and you might question yourself, but don't question God. While you are trying to figure it out, God has already worked it out. God has the solution, and He has strategically placed the right person in your life to help you for such a time as this. You are at the edge of a miracle. Your door is about to swing open with mercy and goodness, and grace is about to kick in. Better days are ahead of you. Joy bells are ringing. Your strength is renewed. Happy days are here again. Everything you thought was dead will come alive, and your dry bones will quicken. Watch God turn around in your favor what was meant for evil. "God knows the thoughts that he thinks toward you. Thoughts of peace and not of evil to give you an expected end." (Jeremiah 29:11). Therefore, sit back, relax, and enjoy the favor of God on your life. It's your time to blossom, shine, and come out of the darkness into the marvelous light (1 Peter 2:9).

You can't quit because you are tired and weary; away with the complaints, whining, and murmuring. "Greater is he that is in you, than he that is in the world" (1 John 4:4). Perhaps you are tired of believing, tired of another prophecy. I've been there. Tired of waiting. I've been there. Tired of struggling. I've been there. Tired of being sick and tired. I've been there too. I almost gave up, but giving up is not an option. That is what the enemy wants you to do so that he can destroy the followers of Jesus. "The thief comes to steal, and kill, and destroy; but I have come that you may have life and have it more abundantly" (John 10:10). Only you can fight for the breakthrough to your miracle. Only you can give birth to your dreams. Yes, the battle belongs to God; however, you must do your part. It's a two-way street. Only you can fight to fulfill your dreams. No one else can do it for you. God will give you strength when you have none of your own. Remember, when Moses' arms got tired, God placed Joshua (Moses' successor) and Hur there to hold his arms up. When you fall short, He will pick you up, turn you around, and place your feet on solid ground. Isaiah 40:29 declares, "He will give strength to the weary and increase the power of the weak" so that you won't give up! You are now on the verge of a breakthrough.

Anyone who lifts weights knows that the most difficult times of weight training are the moments right before the final reps when the muscles are beginning to fatigue. You are tired and exhausted beyond what you can endure, and the last thing you want to hear from the Personal Trainer is to push. You can't take it anymore! You have pushed, pushed, and exhausted all of your strength. You don't have another push in you. You want to scream, "I can't do this! I can't!" But, you must. It is at this time that you must push the hardest and exert yourself the most. You are crying, "I can't" while everyone around you is yelling, "Push!" Easy for them to say, they are not the one going through all the pain! Yet, you know they are right; you have to push. Then, somewhere deep inside of you gets a second wind. At this point, you now have determination where hopelessness used to dwell and you can proclaim boldly, "I can do all things through Christ Jesus who strengthens me" (Philippians 4:13).

The Bible says in Job 22:28, "Thou shall declare a thing, and it will be established unto thee." I declare in the name of Jesus that you will be blessed with God's supernatural wisdom and a clear direction for living. You will be blessed with creativity, vision, and abundance. You will be blessed with self-control and self-discipline. You will be blessed with a great family, good friends, and good health. You will be blessed with faith, favor, and fulfillment. You will be blessed with promotion, supernatural strength, and divine protection. You will be blessed with a compassionate heart, and a positive outlook on life. "You will be blessed in the city, and in the country. Blessed shalt thou be when you comest in, and blessed shalt thou be when thou goest out" (Deuteronomy 28:3; 28:6). "You will be the lender, and not the borrower. You will be the head, and not the tail." (Deuteronomy 28:12-13).

I declare and decree that everything you put your hands on this year, and the coming years, will prosper beyond your expectations. I declare and decree that all things are possible. Be strong and don't give up.

DECLARATION OF OWNERSHIP (VI)

THE POWER OF I AM
*Who shall separate us from the love of Christ?
Shall tribulation, or distress, or persecution or
famine, or nakedness, or peril, or sword?*
Romans 8:35

I AM FAR MORE THAN RUBIES
*Who can find a virtuous woman?
For her price is far beyond rubies.*
Proverbs 31:10

I AM THE APPLE OF GOD'S EYE
*For thus said the Lord of hosts, after his glory
has he sent me unto the nations which plundered you:
for he that touches you touches the apple of his eye.*
Zechariah 2:8

I AM FEARFULLY AND WONDERFULLY MADE
*I will praise thee; for I am fearfully and wonderfully made:
marvelous are thy works; and that my soul knoweth right well.*
Psalm 139:14

I AM ROYAL, CHOSEN, AND PECULIAR
*But ye are a chosen generation, a royal priesthood, and a
holy nation, a peculiar people; that ye should
shew forth the praises of him who hath called you out of the
darkness into the marvelous light.*
1 Peter 2:9

I AM LOYAL
Casting all your cars unto him; for he careth for you.
1 Peter 5:7

I AM A SOWER
*Give and it shall be given unto you; good measure, pressed
down, shaken together, running over, shall men give unto
your bosom.*
Luke 6:38

CHAPTER 8
Find Your Why So You Can Fly

I can do all things through Christ, which strengtheneth me.
Philippians 4:13

Have you ever asked yourself, "Why do I exist? Why am I here on Earth? What is my purpose? Why am I sometimes unhappy with my life?" To begin answering those questions, you have to remember that God made you in His own image. You're not a mistake or an accident. When you are struggling with your emotions, you have two choices: sit and cry or do something. Here are concrete steps you can take to overcome challenges and rebuild your life, so that you can find your why and fly, and become as successful as you were meant to be.

The first step in any journey is to acknowledge that you are not living your best life. The restless desire is a sign that your time has come to move from where you are to where you want to be. Novelist Robert Louis Stephenson once said, "To be what we are, and to become what we are capable of becoming, is the only end in life." In other words, the most worthwhile purpose in life is to become oneself, whatever that might mean to you. Listen to your heart's desire and find out what you should do next. God has much more in store for you than you could ever imagine in your wildest dreams. When God told Abraham (father of multitudes, earlier name Abram) to move out of his country, Abram didn't call his "Best Friends Forever" (BFF's) for their opinions. Nor did he say, "God, give me a few days to think about it." What's more, he didn't say, "God, I need to pray about it." He didn't ask his wife Sarah (mother of multitudes, earlier name Sarai) what she thought. Deliberations are sidetracks to get us off our purpose. Sarai called a family meeting with her maidservants informing them of relocation. The maidservants gathered boxes, and packed all the necessary items for the trip. Abram, Sarai, Lot (Abram's nephew), and the maidservants said goodbye to their friends and neighbors, and off they went.

The second step in any journey is realizing that your purpose is not something you desire, it is something you discover. Once you realize your hidden strengths, your weaponry fastens together others in your arsenal, and becomes visible and more resilient with each use. God has placed inside of you everything you need to take the necessary steps. Your gift is not going to fall out of the sky. Your gift is locked up inside of you. No matter what you have been told, what the results were from the test you took, or what you might believe about yourself – you have a unique gift inside of you that can change the world. Understanding what's inside of you is an essential ingredient to finding a sense of purpose in life. In order to attain a true sense of purpose, ask yourself what I call "The What Motivators." These are the essential ingredients that I hold at the core of my being. I try to allow them to govern my purpose in life, helping me to find my why so that I can fly.

Essential Ingredients to Finding Your Purpose in Life:
- *What is your passion? What are your talents? What delights you?*
- *What motivates you? What fires you up? What inspires you?*
- *What leaps in your spirit? What sets your teeth on edge?*
- *What nurtures your inner life? What does your soul thirst for?*

- *What's struggling to be born within you? What's tugging at your heart?*
- *What's your God-given calling?*

Too many people drift through life feeling worthless, hopeless, and unfulfilled. They are doing what they've been told to do, living out someone else's life, and dying with their purpose inside of them. I was definitely one of those people for most of my life. But now, I am stronger, wiser, and living life on purpose. Embracing the gift that's inside of you can give you a sense of being able to do the impossible. After all, the purpose of life is to live it, taste it, and pursue your dreams.

The third step in any journey is to believe in yourself. If you are not sure about your next move or which direction to go in, ask God. He is your Abba Father, and He always has your best interest at heart. He will never leave you. He is with you right now, even as your eyes read through the text on this page. No matter what you are facing, He knows your need. Ask, seek, and knock (Matthew 7:7), the door is open to His heart. Believe in yourself, and what God has placed in you will happen. If you don't believe in yourself, no one else will. You don't need intelligence or opportunity to believe in yourself. The biggest difference between believers and nonbelievers (in health, in business, and in life) is that believers are determined to pursue their dreams in spite of obstacles and fear. Fear is false evidence appearing real. Expose yourself to your deepest fear; after that, fear will have no power. It will shrink and vanish.

Several years ago, I had a frightening experience in my home when I went to use the toilet. Usually I don't look before I sit; but, this time I did. To my surprise, there was a mouse in the toilet bowl. As I began to squat, the mouse looked up at me as if I was invading his space and I was to wait my turn. I took a few steps forward, just enough to turn my back to the toilet, and screamed at the top of my lungs. I was paralyzed with fear! My husband, Ron, jumped up from his recliner in the family room, and ran to see why I was screaming. I explained my fear to him, but received no sympathy, just a good scolding about the fact that I didn't put the lid down to trap the mouse or flush it down the toilet. Everyone is afraid of something, big or small. Eventually, you will have to deal with your fear. No fear can ever defeat you unless you allow it. Don't let fear hinder you from fulfilling your purpose in life. Do it afraid!

DECLARATION OF OWNERSHIP (VII)

THE POWER OF I AM
Also I heard the voice of the Lord, saying, Whom shall I send, and who will go for us? Then said I, Here am I; send me.
Isaiah 6:8

I AM A SERVANT OF GOD
And in very deed for this cause have I raised thee up, for to shew in thee my power; and that my name may be declared throughout all the earth.
Exodus 9:16

I AM HIS WORKMANSHIP
I know that thou canst do everything, and that no thought can be witholden from thee.
Job 42:2

I AM IN HIS COUNSEL
There are many devices in a man's heart; nevertheless the counsel of the Lord, that shall stand.
Proverbs 19:21

I AM DRIVEN BY PURPOSE
Counsel in the heart of man is like deep water; but a man of understanding will draw it out.
Proverbs 20:5

I AM WORKING ON ME
Wherefore my beloved, as ye have always obeyed, not as in my presence only, but now much more in my absence, work out your own soul salvation with fear and trembling. For it is God which worketh in you both to will and to do of his good pleasure.
Philippians 2:12-13

I AM CALLED
And we know that all things work together for good to them that love God, to them who are the called according to his purpose.
Romans 8:28

CHAPTER 9
A Date with Destiny

*And the angel came in unto her, and said,
Hail, thou that art highly favoured, the Lord is with
thee: blessed art thou among women.*
Luke 1:28

Promises, promises, and more promises. Honoring promises is high on my list of requirements. By giving your word, one can be assured that your promise will be kept. I know emergencies happen; however, when someone fails to follow through on a promise, it registers as a lack of integrity and character. If you have been stood up, then you know what I am talking about. Granted, people do have the right to change their minds from time to time. It's understandable that occasionally circumstances arise after the fact that make following through on a commitment impossible. But if you renege on your promise, then you are a person who lacks integrity. James 1:8 says, "A double-minded man is unstable in all his ways."

A few years ago, I had a person break their word to me. I would have preferred for the person to have said no in the first place so that I would not have felt embarrassed. It is upsetting for a person to break a promise at the last minute. Bear in mind though that God is not like people. If He has made you a promise, He will bring it to pass. People however, are like cars on the freeway; they come and go. They will be with you one minute and against you the next. As a matter of fact, you might be going through a lot of resistance, hostility, and conflict with people right now. But, don't let others diminish your vision, your dream, your desires, or who you are. Some people will exclude you; but, don't feel ostracized, banished, ignored, or snubbed. Jesus said, "But many that are first shall be last; and the last shall be first" (Matthew 19:30).

I am reminded of the Christmas song, "Rudolph the Red Nosed Reindeer." I love this story of exclusion. As a matter of fact, I can relate to Rudolph. I hold him in the highest regard. When you are poles apart from others, sometimes you are treated as an outsider. Rudolph was intimidated and tormented by the other reindeer. They made fun of him, called him names, and would not let him join in their reindeer games. Most people know at least one person who fits the profile of Rudolph. How unlikely: a deer that seems to muddle up relationships and struggle with social interactions because of a malady he was born with. This Christmas song made me reflect back on my high school yearbook. In the back of the yearbook was the name and picture of a graduate most likely to succeed because of their scholastic achievements. Then, there were the rest of us.

Jesus told the story of a wealthy man who was leaving on a long trip. He called his servants together and gave each a measure of money. The man gave five bags of silver to one, two bags of silver to another, and one bag of silver to the last; dividing it according to their abilities. In his absence, one servant invested wisely, and turned his five bags into ten. The other took the two bags, and turned them into four. The last person took his single bag, and buried it in the ground (Matthew 25:16). One of the first things we can learn from this story is that not all people have the same abilities, but each one of us has abilities and we are responsible for using them.

As a person with underdeveloped abilities, who was not voted most likely to succeed, I worked very hard.

Passionate about getting a college degree, I ended up very successful in life. On the other hand, I have seen others who had talent, ability, and everything going their way, yet they squandered it all. Whether you have great talents or only a few, use what you have. If you are faithful over those few things, God will make you a ruler over many (Matthew 25:23). We need to remember that He is our distributor. He has a way of multiplying the little you have if you are faithful.

The Rudolph story is unique. Santa Claus saw something in him that Rudolph did not see in himself. Rudolph with a glowing, red nose is illustrated as the leading reindeer pulling Santa's sleigh on Christmas Eve. The brightness of his nose was so grand it illuminated the team's path through inclement weather. In the same manner, as a child of The Most High God, "Ye are the light of the world. A city that is set on a hill cannot be hidden. Let your light so shine before men, that they may see your good works, and glorify your Father which is in heaven" (Matthew 5:14; 16). Jesus said, "Ye have not chosen me, but I have chosen you, and ordained you, that ye should go and bear fruit, and that your fruit, should remain: that whatsoever ye shall ask of the Father in my name, he may give you" (John 15:16).

In the following pages of this chapter, I want to share a list of essential points that will encourage you to fulfill your date with destiny, which is a self-revealing experience. This list will give you several strategic steps and push you to execute them with clarity and confidence.

Step 1. Diehard Determination.
"And Jesus said unto him, 'No man, having put his hand to the plough, and looking back, is fit for the

kingdom of God'" (Luke 9:62). Often, we know what to do to achieve the life we want, but we still aren't able to make it happen. One of the reasons is because we give up too soon. No one ever said that achieving your dreams would be easy. In fact, it's a difficult path. That's why most people fail to live the life they want. C. S. Lewis (a British Theologian) said, "The only people who achieve much are those who want knowledge so badly that they seek while the conditions are still unfavorable. Favorable conditions never come." Could it be that you need to renew your mind? You have heard the phrase "Just Do It"; in addition, you need to stick to it because things will get rough as you pursue your goals. Have you ever wanted something so badly that you think about it day and night, to the point where it frustrates you? Have you ever been driven? I mean, so truly driven that you will shut some things down to accomplish your goal? You will shut the television down. You will shut your Facebook account down. You will shut some friends down. You will even think about shutting church down for a while because your focus is on completing your goals.

Biblical figure Nehemiah was instrumental in the rebuilding and reestablishment of the Jerusalem Wall. He had a goal; he was determined to complete the task. And because of his diehard determination, he did just that. If you have not gotten anything I've said thus far, get this: "Stay on the Wall." If possible, finish what you have started. Don't come down until you complete your mission. God will give you encouragement and perseverance. "Be confident of this very thing, that he which hath begun a good work in you will perform it until the day of Jesus Christ" (Philippians 1:6).

"The Lord is full of compassion, and is merciful" (Psalm 145:8). So, "you will not be sluggish, but imitators of those who through faith and patience inherit the promise" (Hebrews 6:12). Therefore, "Let patience have her perfect work, so that ye may be perfect and complete, and wanting nothing" (James 1:4). "Cast not away therefore your confidence, which has great recompense of reward" (Hebrews 10:35). God will not fail you or forsake you. No devil on Earth or devil in hell can stop you. No one can stop what He has started, ordained, and put His stamp of approval on. No voodoo or hoodoo can stop God's favor on your life.

Step 2. Dump Distractions.
"Remember Lot's wife" (Luke 17:32). Distractions are interruptions designed to get you off track. Two of the biggest distractions are: artificial thoughts and unproductive habits. They have the propensity to derail you from your assignment. I am easily distracted. I am not sure I could work from home because there are too many distractions. The telephone is a distraction. The television is a distraction. The refrigerator is a distraction. And as informative as the computer is, it can be a distraction. I turn on the computer to do one thing and find myself surfing the Internet. Distractions are nuisances and impediments that keep you from doing what you have purposed in your mind to do.

According to Dr. Mehmet Oz, a cardiac surgeon, author, and host of the Dr. Oz Show, distractions can be annoying even disruptive especially for those who are easily distracted to begin with. Distractions can make it hard to get anything done especially for people with attention deficit hyperactivity disorder (ADHD). But, distractions have an "upside" too; they can provide important clues to your passion. If you find your daily routine interrupted by several distractions, think about translating them into hobbies, interests, or even career opportunities. In a journal, make a list of five distractions. Give each one an entire page. Write the distractions at the top of the page then list five jobs, activities or hobbies you can begin in order to build on your distractions. For example, if you love sports you can join a team or coach little league. If you ever wondered how to become a paid writer, www.write.com is the site for you. Write down the specific skills you are gaining by pursuing your distractions.

A few years ago, I held down three part-time jobs and school. I was very determined to be the first one in my family to graduate with a college degree. It wasn't easy at the age of sixty plus, but I was determined to not let any distractions seize my moment for a higher education. It's time out for "ifs, ands, and buts." It's time to work your dreams. Needless to say, if it had not been for the Lord who was on my side where would I be? I also have the support of my husband who loves me, pushes me, believes in me, and is there to help me.

Step 3. Decide To Put Your Faith Into Action.
"I can do all things through Christ Jesus, which strengtheneth me" (Philippians 4:13). I have made a conscious decision that dreams and goals are worth attaining. In order to do so, I have to work smart and hard. I also realize that I am not the smartest, fastest or the most articulate person in the world, but this will never stop me because I have a date with destiny. I refuse to acknowledge that my limitations are anything but self-imposed. I refuse to let people put limitations on me. "Greater is he that's in you, than he that is in the world" (1 John 4:4). I've learned that if I work hard

and stay focused in the midst of adversity, dreams do eventually come true.

In President Theodore Roosevelt's famous 1910 speech, *The Man in the Arena*, he puts it better than I ever can: "It's not the critic who counts; not the man who points out how the strong man stumbles, or where the doer of deeds could have done them better." The credit belongs to the man who is actually in the arena, whose face is marred by dust and sweat and blood, who strives vigilantly, who errs, who comes short again and again. There is no effort without error and shortcoming. The one who knows the triumph of high achievement is the one who actually strives to do the deeds, who knows great enthusiasm and great devotion, and who spends himself to a worthy cause. At worst, if he fails, at least he fails while daring greatly.

I have spent a lot of time trying to make some sense out of what success means to me. Now, I can truly say that success is not being rich and famous. My success lies in the hurdles I have overcome while trying to succeed. "For what shall it profit a man, if he gains the whole world, and loses his soul" (Mark 8:36). It doesn't matter if you have more or less skills, charisma, and talent than the next person. It doesn't matter at all whether you come from a rich or poor background. It certainly doesn't matter whether you are an F, D, B, C, or A student in school. What matters is daring to have dreams and working hard to achieve them. Yes, you might fail the first time, but if you dare to hang on, you will eventually succeed.

Dare to dream and work to win, but remember to be successful you must BE RELENTLESS. Don't listen to the part of the brain that fears failure. If you value your dreams in any way, you have to give them a fair chance to succeed. What's a little hard work in the pursuit of your dreams? I don't want to be the person on my deathbed looking back at my life wondering what might have been if I had only tried. There may be days when you get up in the morning, and things aren't the way you had hoped they would be. Those are the times to keep your thoughts focused; believe in yourself and all that you are capable of doing. You are your biggest cheerleader. Belief is not just a casual word you mention on occasion to yourself or to someone else. It's your lifeline. It's like breathing. It is crucial to staying alive. It is easy to say, "I believe," but until you put your belief into action, nothing is accomplished. Believing in yourself is your divine connection to your date with destiny.

DECLARATION OF OWNERSHIP (VIII)

THE POWER OF I AM
*For I know the thoughts that I think toward you,
saith the Lord, thoughts of peace, and not of evil,
to give you an expected end.*
Jeremiah 29:11

I AM BORN WITH A PLAN
*But he is unchangeable, and who can turn him back?
What he desires that he does.*
Job 23:13

I AM STEADFAST
*The Lord will perfect that which concerneth me:
thy mercy, O Lord, endureth forever: forsake
not the works of thine own hands.*
Psalm 138:8

I AM PERSISTENT
*Therefore, my beloved brethren, be ye steadfast,
unmovable, always abounding in the work of
the Lord, forasmuch as ye know that your labour
is not in vain in the Lord.*
I Corinthians 15:58

I AM FULLY PERSUADED
*For I am persuaded, that neither death, nor life,
nor angels, nor principalities, nor powers,
nor things present, nor things to come, Nor height,
nor depth, nor any other creature, shall be able to separate
us from the love of God.*
Romans 8:38-39

I AM OPEN AND RECEPTIVE TO HIS WORD
*So shall my word be that goeth forth out of my mouth:
It shall not return unto me void, but it shall accomplish
That which I please, and it shall prosper in the thing
whereto I sent it.*
Isaiah 56:11

I AM COMMITTED TO MY VISION

For the vision is yet for an appointed time, but at the end it shall speak, and not lie: though it tarry, wait for it; because it will surely come it will not tarry.
Habakkuk 2:3

CHAPTER 10
Find Opportunity in Rejection

*When my father and my mother forsake me,
then the Lord will take me up.*
Psalm 27:10

Have you ever felt a terrible feeling in the pit of your stomach when you ask someone for something, and they reject you? It's the beginning of a quiet storm brewing in your spirit. Every human being on Earth has suffered in some form or another from rejection. Rejection is the result of a failure to reach a standard or expectation – what we do is not good enough. Some of the side effects of being rejected are anger, resentment, and dislike. Not internalizing rejection is a skill you can learn, just like any other coping skill. For instance, learn how not to put yourself in a place where you can be rejected. Learn not to accept everything that is dished out to you; lessening your chances of becoming a victim of other people's needs, desires, and wants.

Learn to embrace rejection as an opportunity not opposition. Do you remember the story of Joseph in Genesis 37? Joseph's father, Jacob, had twelve sons; but, he favored and loved his eleventh son, Joseph, the most. Do you recall that his brothers were jealous of him? When Jacob presented Joseph with a beautiful, multi-colored coat, the eleven elder brothers sold Joseph into slavery, telling their father that Joseph was dead. They thought, "Here comes Joseph, the dreamer, who thinks he is better than everybody else. Let's teach him a lesson and get rid of him." Joseph is a great example of a person who was rejected.

Moses, "The Great Deliverer" of the Israelites, had the same problem. In Exodus 2, Moses killed the Egyptian because he was trying to help his own people. Moses was sent to be their ruler and deliverer by God himself; but, those very people rejected him with these words, "Who made you ruler and judge?" (Acts7:35).

Saul, the first king of Israel, rejected David (a man after God's own heart) as the next king. Though Saul admitted to knowing that David should be the next king, he did not turn the kingdom over to the young man. David spent most of his twenties running for his life because Saul continually tried to hunt him down and kill him. He even mentioned that his own mother and father had rejected him (Psalm 27:10). Oh, what a feeling to be rejected. But, from rejection these three ordinary men became extraordinary leaders.

When Jesus returned to his hometown of Nazareth, His own people rejected him. After hearing testimonies of healing, deliverance, and miracles from others all over the world, the people of Nazareth still doubted and discredited Him. They could not believe that this son of a carpenter could be preaching, "Repent the Kingdom of Heaven is near" (Matthew 4:17). Isaiah 53:3 says, "He was despised and rejected by men; a man of sorrows, and familiar with suffering." Jesus concluded, "No prophet is accepted in his own town" (Luke 4:24). So if you have ever felt rejection, welcome to the Jesus club. In other words, we are in good company with those in the Bible. Despite the discouragement, pain, and rejection, Jesus continued what God the Father had commissioned Him to do; He spread the good news of love, forgiveness, and salvation. His experience of being rejected did not discourage Him from continuing His ministry. Jesus said, "I am the way, the truth, and the life: no man can come unto the Father, but by me" (John 14:6).

A great time to reinvent yourself or devise another action plan is while you are experiencing rejection. Les Brown, motivational speaker and author, once said, "If you want to keep on getting what you are getting, keep on doing what you are doing." In other words, what you are doing is not working – it's time to try something different. A few years ago, I was feeling frustrated. Many things in my life didn't seem to be progressing as I had hoped, and I felt like I was getting nowhere. I decided to take charge of my life and do what really matters to me. Change is a constant, so make sure that you're constantly assessing what's working and what is not so that you can move forward. Don't allow yourself to be stuck. If something's not working, stop forcing it. Try something different.

Recently, I have come to the realization that it is alright to say no. As Oprah Winfrey explains, "Finding yourself is not about what you add to your life, it's about what you can take away." Once you have created your absolute yes list (the top priorities in your life), it becomes easier to identify those things that you'll need to let go.

Rejection is like a bad toothache. You have to rid yourself of the pain because the aching tooth has no value to you. The sooner you get over the pain, the sooner you will feel better. Rejection can be a problem if you let someone tie it to your self-worth. For instance, if rejection in your eyes means that you didn't get what you wanted, you will feel unworthy. Get over yourself. It has nothing to do with your self-worth. Rejection helps us to weed out the old and bring in the new. Rejection is nothing more than a necessary step in the pursuit of a new opportunity.

Let's be real, everyone is not going to like you. As a matter of fact, the Bible says, "Beware when everyone speaks well of you" (Luke 6:26). Also, ignore the naysayer who tells you that you can't do this, that, or the other. Sometimes people will try to discourage you because you live a purpose-driven life. When there is purpose in life, there are no safety zones. You will go against all odds despite many struggles. The more you strive the more you will want to strive.

Embrace every opportunity. If someone rejects you, respect their request, and wish them only good in life. You do not need to completely avoid them, but they are not a necessity in your life. This doesn't mean you should hate them. It will bring God pleasure for you to wish good for others rather than to hate them. Hatred inflicts pain on your own life. God does not want us to live frustrated and miserable lives. Listen to Him, abide in His Word, and trust Him when you can't trace Him, even if He seems far away.

Just as you cannot hear the other person in a conversation if you are talking or if your mind is distracted, so it is with God. Before you can hear Him, you must be ready to listen. If you want to hear Him speak, you must be quiet and you must be focused on what He is saying. Regular conversation with God can transform your life! Consider identifying a place and time to meet with Him every day.

Transforming your perception of rejection begins with developing a new way of thinking and new habits. Come up with ways to challenge yourself. Become actively engaged with people and ideas. For some of us that means volunteering. Instead of asking yourself, "What will make me happy?" the better question is, "What will offer me more fulfillment?" You do not have to suffer or endure your way through life. We often base our lives on the future, telling ourselves that we are going to be happy when the kids move out, when we retire, or when we get out of debt. But, it is unwise to wait for everything to be perfect before you decide to enjoy your life.

Enjoyment is never attained by how well you have paved the way for it or how well you can justify having earned it. True enjoyment is not a conditional experience: it is a birthright, a possession, and a privilege. You have the right to have peace and enjoyment in your life. Live the life that is best for you no matter what the world thinks. Dare to get out of your comfort zone. Take on a task that will test you. Opportunity requires risk and challenges. More than anything, you must believe in yourself like never before or you will never get from A to Z. If you do not come out of your safety nest and flap your wings, you will never learn how to fly and soar. Think big in a small place, and don't sweat small beginnings. If you are faithful over few things,

God will make you ruler over many (Matthew 25:23). You are destined to reign and rule over what God has entrusted to you. He has given you His stamp of approval; signed, sealed, and delivered. All you have to do is step out of doubt and into faith. God has selected you to be His treasured possession. "You are a chosen generation, a royal priesthood, a holy nation…" (1 Peter 2:9).

As aforementioned, David was rejected by Saul, but chosen by God to be the next king of Israel. God told Samuel (the priest) that He had chosen someone to be the king of Israel, and Samuel was to go and visit a family in Bethlehem. While he was there, God would tell him whom it was He had chosen to be king. Samuel went to the town of Bethlehem, and visited a man named Jesse. He asked to see Jesse's sons, and one by one they all came in to stand in front of him. First, the eldest son, Eliab, came in. He was tall, strong, and good-looking. Samuel thought to himself, "This has to be the one that God has chosen!" But, no, it wasn't! God said to Samuel, "Don't think about how good he looks or how tall he is, he isn't the one I want. I don't look at things that people look at; I take notice of what is in someone's heart" (1 Samuel 16:7). The next two sons came in and God didn't choose either of them; then the next one, and the next one, and on and on until he had seen all seven sons. Samuel didn't anoint any of them. Then, there were no more. He was a little bit puzzled and asked Jesse, "Are these all of your sons?" Jessie responded, "Well, no. These aren't all of my sons. The youngest one is out looking after the sheep." "*Hold dinner. No one will sit down and eat until we find God's chosen king*," Samuel implored (1 Samuel 16:11, emphasis added).

Soon, David arrived. He was ruddy and had a beautiful countenance (he was good to look at). God said to Samuel, "Arise and anoint him: this is the one I want to be the King over Israel" (1 Samuel 16:12). I sense in my spirit that God is saying the same to you, "Arise, and shine!" You are the one, for such a time as this, who will be used by God for His glory. So, Samuel picked up his ram's horn that was full of oil (in those days, they used the horn from an animal to carry things like oil because they didn't have bottles like we have today); then, he poured the oil over David's head (this is what the Bible calls anointing) with all of his family watching. From then on, God was with David. God knew what was in David's heart, and He knew that

David was a man who would love and trust Him (1 Samuel 16: 4-13).

"Life and death are in the power of the tongue" (Proverbs 18:21). Life is unpredictable, so embrace it. When you are rejected say, "Next!" and keep it moving. Use the opposition to create a new adventure and a new you. If you correct your mind, the rest of your life will fall into place. I have come to the understanding that change is constant. King David was a man after God's own heart. Moses was "The Great Deliverer" of the Israelites. Joseph was an innocent victim who was betrayed by his brothers. Nevertheless, each one of those men found opportunity in opposition.

The sting of rejection can be painful. However, the sting of that pain is not unto death. Pain has its promises. Just about everyone has heard of the suffering of Job in the Old Testament. He had it all: a large family, wealth, and blessings of every kind imaginable. Then, he lost it all without understanding why. Subsequently, his health began to deteriorate. His wife told him to curse God and commit suicide, but he remained strong and faithful. Through it all, Job did not sin nor did he blame God. Job didn't understand why he had to undergo so much pain; nevertheless, he trusted God. God then brought him to this understanding: believers don't always know what God is doing in their lives. In the end, Job answered God by saying, "I have declared what I didn't understand" (Job 42:3). God then blessed Job with twice as much as he had before his trials began.

God turned Job's situation around for his good. Job didn't lose hope and give up on life. In the same manner, God can turn a bad situation around in your life. However, your faith must be rooted and grounded in Him. God is not a respecter of persons, but He is a respecter of faith. "And without faith, it is impossible to please him: for he that comes to God must believe that he is a rewarder of them that diligently seek him" (Hebrews 11:6). Seek God with your whole heart, mind, body, soul, and spirit. Talk to Him, and He will give you rest for your weary soul. You've talked to everyone else, but have you talked to God? Lift up your head, square your shoulders, stick out your chest, reach down into your Holy Ghost bank account, and make a withdrawal of fortitude. Walk in fortitude in the face of rejection; facing all challenges with strength, confidence, and courage. Courage is when you continue on even though it seems that the odds are against you. Courageously continue the good fight of faith.

Rejection is often the most difficult obstacle an individual must face and overcome. But, rejection often leads to change. Change has been compared to a snowball rolling down a slope. As it continues on its path, it gathers energy; growing bigger and more powerful. Progress does not come without change. "Many resist change, perhaps even fear it, but the best ones know how to find opportunities in rejection, and they seize the moment." – Author Unknown

DECLARATION OF OWNERSHIP (IX)

THE POWER OF I AM
My grace is sufficient for thee: for my strength is made perfect in weakness.
2 Corinthians 12:9

I AM FULFILLING MY DREAMS
I can do all things through Christ who strengtheneth me.
Philippians 4:13

I AM AN OVERCOMER
The Lord is my strength and my shield; my heart trusted in him, and I am helped: therefore my heart greatly rejoiceth; and and with my son will I praise him.
Psalm 27:7

I AM CLIMBING ABOVE EVERY OBSTACLE
He giveth power to the faint: and to them that have no might he increaseth strength.
Isaiah 40:29

I AM SOARING TO NEW HEIGHTS
But those who wait upon the Lord shall renew their strength; they shall mount up with wings as eagles; they shall run, and not be weary; and they shall walk, and not faint.
Isaiah 40:31

I AM LEANING ON HIM
The Lord is good, a stronghold in the day of trouble and he knoweth them that trust in him.
Nahum 1:7

I AM STEPPING OUT OF MY COMFORT ZONE
Be strong and of a good courage, fear not, nor be afraid of them: for the LORD thy God, he it is that doth go with thee; he will not fail thee, nor forsake thee.
Deuteronomy 31:6

CHAPTER 11
Determined to Keep on Going

*These things I have spoken unto you,
that in me ye might have peace.
In the world ye might have tribulation:
but be of good cheer; I have overcome the world.
John 16:33*

Have you ever faced a loss or felt devastated by an outcome? It may have been due to the passing away of loved ones, the loss of a job, or it might have been the loss of a home to foreclosure. Perhaps even the loss of a business venture or a business investment due to a weak economy.

It is easy to become discouraged – if you allow yourself to dwell on things that make you angry. Life can be overwhelming and unpredictable. There are scores of people in the Bible who went through some (if not all) of the things we have encountered.

The Apostle Paul's influence on Christianity was second only to Jesus Christ. Paul spread the gospel throughout The Roman Empire, and wrote thirteen books of the New Testament. Paul was regularly attacked because of his faith, but Jesus stood by him and spoke these comforting words of encouragement, "In the world you shall have tribulation: but be of good cheer; I have overcome the world" (John 16:33). Evidently, Paul was greatly discouraged along the way. Not one of us makes it through life without problems, challenges, and sometimes tragedies.

There are many individuals who have faced difficulties, and have persevered because of their faith in God. "The just shall live by faith" (Hebrews 10:38).

God has not brought us this far to leave us as orphans; therefore, remain determined to walk in faith not in fear.

A word of caution: when you are determined to keep on going, Satan will raise his ugly head to find something or someone to discourage you. Don't be ignorant of his devices. Be alert. Satan is tricky. He is scheming and plotting a way to trip you up, and make you give up. Satan is a liar. Remember, life is like boxing. It is not about how hard you're hit. The question is, can you take a hit and keep on going? I am reminded of the song, "I Believe I Can Fly" by R. Kelly. Indulge me while I share the lyrics: *"I used to think that I could not go on. And life was nothing but an awful song. But now I know the meaning of true love. I'm leaning on the everlasting arms. If I can see it, then I can do it. If I just believe it, there's nothing to it. I believe I can fly. I believe I can touch the sky. I think about it every night and day. Spread my wings and fly away. I believe I can soar. I see me running through that open door... See I was on the verge of breaking down. Sometimes silence can seem so loud. There are miracles in life I must achieve. But first I know it starts inside of me... I believe I can fly!"*

God has revealed many signs and wonders to me. He wants me to please Him by walking in love and faith, striving to stay sweet, staying prayerful, repenting of my sins, and remaining willing to forgive and turn the other cheek even if it doesn't feel good. Now that may seem like a lot to give of myself, but He so loved the world that He gave His only begotten son that I might have life, and have it more abundantly. I am so glad that He freely paid the price that bought my redemption. I am so glad that I can go to Him when I am feeling down and out. He is my refuge, and my rock. When my burdens are heavy, He will strengthen me. When my heart is broken, He will comfort me. "Nay, in all these things we are more than conquerors through him who loved us (Romans 8:37)." I am determined to keep on going. I will finish my assignment. What about you?

When you are facing harsh conditions, hard times, and health issues remember child of God, have faith in God because "Greater is he that is in you, than he that is in the world (1 John 4:4)." "Thanks be unto God who causes us to triumph in all circumstances" (2 Corinthians 2:14).

Therefore, count your blessings, and not your problems. Trust me, you can push through the valley of the shadow of death by renewing your mind with the Word of God. You can push through obstacles, challenges, and adversity. The Bible instructs us in Mark 11:23 to speak to our mountain: "For truly I say unto you, that whoever shall say to this mountain, be you moved, and be ye cast into the sea; and shall not doubt in his heart, but shall believe that what he says will come to pass; he shall have it." Let me share with you three vital things that will strengthen your determination to keep on going.

Number one: *Be your own cheerleader*. Life is like a seesaw, chock-full of ups and downs. It will take everything inside of you (and then some) to keep on going. It takes determination, and a lot of it. The odds indicate that most of us will quit because of delayed gratification and suffering. But, push through. No one will do it for you. King David was in great distress, but the Bible says that he encouraged himself. Tony Robbins, author and motivational speaker says, "Life happens not to me, but for me." Frame your actions by your deeds not by your words. Faith without works is dead. Just do something. In other words, be possessed with passion coupled with action.

Number two: *Be aware of distractions.* Distractions break our concentration and lower our productivity. It doesn't matter where you are, you probably deal with distractions daily. What's more, regaining concentration after a distraction can take a few minutes. Some of the most common distractions we face are emails. Many of us can spend the entire day merely reading and responding to them. Also, browsing the web can take an enormous amount of time from our day. When I start looking on the internet for one thing, it's easy to get lost for 60 minutes or more. A cell phone often creates the greatest distraction. Even if you go all day without touching it, just having it near you may distract you from a simple task. You probably already know what distracts you the most – emails, browsing the internet, cell phones, and so on; so, limit the amount of time you spend checking emails, never browse the web when you are short on time, and reduce the amount of time you spend talking on your cell phone. (I will address distractions more in chapter fifteen).

Number three: *Be the person you want to become.* True inner power comes from believing that the source of all you desire is within you. All of us have untouched talents, unused abilities, and unidentified gifts waiting to be discovered. God wants us to peel away the layers we try to hide behind, and eradicate the excuses we use as camouflage. Doing so will reveal our true beauty. When you discover your gift and take action, you will begin to live outside the box. If the person you want to become depends on you pleasing people, you will never become the person you want to be. Let go of what people might think about you. You have to rise above the crowd in order to see the big picture.

When Jesus was passing through Jericho, Zacchaeus (a chief tax collector) wished very much to see Him. Being short in stature, he had to rise above the crowd; so, Zacchaeus climbed a sycamore tree. Jesus paused beneath that very tree, and looking up urged Zacchaeus to come down for He had decided to stay at his house. Zacchaeus hurried down gladly, and invited Jesus to his home. From that day on, his life was changed (Luke 19:1-10). If you are going to be a game changer and a history maker, you must divorce yourself from the crowd and stay married to your purpose. "Be steadfast, unmovable, always abounding in the work of the Lord, forasmuch as ye know, that your labour is not in vain in the Lord" (1 Corinthians 15:58). I pray that you stay determined to keep on going, determined to stay on course, determined to stay strong in the Lord and the power of His might, determined to fight the good fight of faith, and determined to believe in the impossible.

DECLARATION OF OWNERSHIP (X)

THE POWER OF I AM
*I have set the Lord always before me; because
he is at my right hand; I shall not be moved.*
Psalm 16:8

I AM RENEWING MY MIND
*I beseech you therefore brethren, by the mercies of
God that ye present your bodies a living sacrifice, holy,
acceptable unto God, which is your reasonable service.*
Romans 12:1

*And be not conformed to this world:
but be ye transformed by the renewing of your mind, that ye
may prove what is the good and acceptable, and perfect,
will of God.*
Romans 12:2

I AM IN IT TO WIN IT
*Know ye not that they which run in a race run all,
but one receiveth the prize? So run, that ye may obtain.*
1 Corinthians 9:24

*And every man that striveth for the mastery is
temperate in all things. Now they do it to obtain
a corruptible crown; but we an incorruptible.*
1 Corinthians 9:25

*I therefore so run, not as uncertainly;
so fight I, not as one that beaten the air.*
1 Corinthians 9:26

*But I keep under my body, and bring it into
subjection; lest that by any means, when I have
preached to others, I myself should be a castaway.*
1 Corinthians 9:26

I AM PRESSING FORWARD
*I can do all things through Christ
who strengtheneth me.*
Philippians 4:13

*I fought a good fight, I have finished my course,
I have kept the faith:*
2 Timothy 4:7

Behold, the people shall rise up as a great lion, and lift up himself as a young lion: he shall not lie down until he eat of the prey, and drink the blood of the slain.
Numbers 23:24

CHAPTER 12
Your Best Is Within Reach

Brethren, I count not myself to have apprehended:
But this one thing I do, forgetting those things, which are
behind, and reaching forth
unto those things which are before.
Philippians 3:13

We know that life can be overwhelming at times. But, despite the challenges, I believe that purpose can be found in your pain. As you prepare for your journey, you must take an in-depth look at your life by digging down deep into your nucleus, the control center of your DNA. Dig deeper into your core, no matter how painful a situation might be, always looking for truth. Truth is the place where your transformation begins.

Think of it like this. Your core is much like laying a foundation for a building. If the foundation becomes unstable, the building becomes weak and falls apart. On most days to strengthen my physical core, I do seven hundred crunches. The Bible instructs us to look inside to experience a transformation. For some of us, we need to work diligently. You must be willing to be honest with yourself and conduct a thorough examination about where you are currently to see if you are in the acceptable will of God. Often, honesty hurts before it heals, but once it heals you find strength in your weakness.

Do you need mental and physical strength? Jesus gives us strength for today. You see, strength for today will not do for tomorrow or next year. We need strength daily. Wasn't it Jesus who taught us to pray? "Give us this day our daily bread" (Matthew 6:11). God in His divine wisdom gives us today's grace for today's needs. He told us not to worry about tomorrow. In Exodus 16:4, the Lord said to Moses, "I will rain down bread from heaven. The people are to go out each day and gather enough for that day."

Am I speaking to someone who feels weak in a particular area? Maybe you're weak physically with sickness. Perhaps you are weak with anxieties, or you are weak in the work place. Maybe your Achilles heel has slipped, and you are in a backslidden condition. Whether you feel weak in your body, mind, soul or spirit, I have good news for you! The very place that you feel weak is the very place God has promised that His strength is made perfect. "The outward man perishes everyday yet the inward man is renewed every day" (2 Corinthians 4:16). Furthermore, the Prophet Isaiah said, "But they that wait upon the Lord he shall renew their strength; they shall mount up with wings as eagles; they shall run, and not be weary; and they shall walk, and not faint" (Isaiah 40:31).

The flesh is a force to be reckoned with. It is always unstable, and it has a mind of its own. The flesh is not nice but naughty. Your flesh will tell you that you are alright where you are rather than push you, promote you, or persuade you in the ways of God. Don't give in to the flesh. Don't sink your teeth into the flesh. Crucify the flesh and bring it under subjection. Change the cycle from "I hope so" to "I know so." Use the gift that is inside of you to leverage your life's purpose. Bear in mind that a purpose without a plan leads to insanity, and without a plan you have no destiny. Destiny does not happen by chance, but by choice. I want to give you a few points that will encourage you to remember that your best is within reach.

Number one: *Don't be lazy.* Lazy people won't pursue anything. They see that you have taken the initiative, and they see the benefits of your labor. Now, they want to ride your coattail. The devil is a liar. The Bible has a great deal to say about laziness. 1) "If anyone desires not to work, neither should he eat" (2 Thessalonians 3:10). 2) "Go to the ant, thou sluggard; consider her ways, and be wise" (Proverbs 6:6). 3) "Not slothful in business; fervent in spirit; serving the Lord" (Romans 12:11). There is no room for laziness in the life of a believer. We cannot be lazy with money management (by living well over our means), in discipleship (by not witnessing; assuming it is someone else's responsibility), or in keeping up with current events (by not knowing what's going on around us).

Number two: *Don't be afraid to fail.* Be afraid not to try. Trying something new opens up the possibility for you to enjoy something new. People who look fear in the face and say, "As long as I am running, fear will not catch up with me" carve their entire careers out. You have an option to stay where you are and be miserable or step up your game. Either you are going forward in growth or stepping back into safety. Trust what is inside of you. Listen to the inward voice and bravely obey it. Don't try to figure it out. Your wants, your struggles, your trials, your afflictions, and your imperfections are molding you. Embrace the journey and trust the process.

Number three: *Don't be afraid to grow.* Growth seems to require that we take action, whether it's a new attitude or a new way of thinking. Trusting yourself in uncharted territory often brings new ideas. There is an innate longing for greatness within all of us. The longing can never be fulfilled without a willingness to change, improve, and try something new. Become so wrapped up in something that you forget to be afraid. You have the power to shape your destiny. Stay positive, stay focused, and surround yourself with like-minded people. Surround yourself with people who have dreams, desires, and ambition. This way you can push each other up the hill. Surround yourself with people who are mentally, spiritually, emotionally, and psychologically strong.

DECLARATION OF OWNERSHIP (XI)

THE POWER OF I AM
*Be strong therefore, and let not your hands
be weak: for your work shall be rewarded.*
Numbers 15:7

I AM FINISHING THE RACE
*God is our refuge and strength, a very present help
in trouble.*
Psalm 46:1

*Our heart is not turned back, neither
have our steps declined from thy way.*
Psalm 44:18

*For the Lord God helps me,
therefore, I am not disgraced; Therefore, I have set
my face like flint, and I know that
I will not be ashamed.*
Isaiah 50:7

I AM NOT STOPPING
But ye, brethren, be not weary in well-doing.
2 Thessalonians 3:13

*So that we see ourselves glory in you
in the churches of God for your patience and faith in
all your persecutions and tribulations
that ye endure.*
2 Thessalonians 1:4

*Wherefore seeing we also are compassed about with
so great a cloud of witnesses,
let us lay aside every weight, and the sin which doth
so easily beset us, and let us run with patience the race that
is set before us.*
Hebrews 12:1

*Know ye not that they, which run in a race,
run all, but one receiveth the prize.
So run that you may obtain.*
1 Corinthians 9:24

I AM LOOKING UPWARD

*I lift mine eyes unto the hills,
from whence cometh my help.
My help cometh from the LORD, which made
heaven and earth. He will not suffer thy foot to be moved:
he that keepeth thee will not slumber.*
Psalm 121:1-3

*That I may know him and the power of his
resurrection and the fellowship of his sufferings, being
conformable unto his death.*
Philippians 3:10

CHAPTER 13
In the Face of Fear

Have I not commanded thee?
Be strong and be of good courage;
be not afraid, neither by thou dismayed: for the Lord thy
God is with thee wheresoever thou goest.
Joshua 1:9

If we are honest, every one of us has some type of fear; but, if your fears prevent you from doing the things that you truly want to do, then you have a serious problem. Don't let fear dictate what you should or should not do. There is some truth in the saying, "Fear is false evidence appearing real." I believe that we as Christians have masqueraded our true feelings about our constant struggles with fear; masking ourselves to prove that we are something we are not. But, you are not The Lone Ranger. It's time to drop the act and ask God to help you with your chronic fear.

Many of the great heroes of faith in the Bible struggled with some type of fear. Nabal was a rich sheep master who insulted King David when he asked him for food for his hungry men. The next morning after Nabal woke up from a drunken stupor and found out what happened, his heart died within and he became like a stone. Nabal died of fear when he heard about King David's threat to take his life (1 Samuel 25: 1-42).

The Biblical story of Gideon is solely about God empowering a man who was paralyzed with fear. Gideon struggled with fear, weakness, and his own insecurities when God chose him to lead the Israelites to victory against the Midianites. He had to be reminded that God was with him (Judges 6:1-40). His story encourages those who have fears that keep them up at night. Today, acknowledge your weakness and allow God to shine in and through you. When you believe that God is your first, last, and only option, you are right where He wants you to be – in His care and trust.

Moses, "The Great Deliverer," had his bout with fear. He had all kinds of excuses as to why he could not be used by God. Moses pled the Fifth Amendment: "I am not a good speaker. I have a speech impediment. I get tongue-tied. My words get all tangled up. The people won't listen to me" (Exodus 4:10).

Other than Nabal, Gideon, and Moses, perhaps Abraham was the most fearful. He told a lie that Sarah was his girlfriend instead of his wife. Also, at 80 years old, Abraham struggled with the fear of not becoming a father. Finally, Abraham's wife Sarah gave birth to Isaac, the promised son. Then, God turned around and told Abraham to offer up his son as a sacrifice. He did it – but not without fear and trembling.

Just like everyone in the Bible, God's strength is made perfect in our weakness. Nabal, Gideon, Moses, and Abraham's stories are also about our fears, our weaknesses, and our insecurities. But, instead of us masquerading our fears, weaknesses, and insecurities, we must see them as keys to unlocking the door of God's strength. Fear anticipates the worst and not the best. What if I get a bad report from the doctor? What if I lose my job? What if I lose my home? What if this? What if that? Often, the things we fear the most never even happen. The devil loves to operate through fear. John 10:10 says, "The thief comes to steal, and to kill, and to destroy."

When it comes to fear, there is no such thing as one size fits all. Fear comes in an assortment of flavors. Nearly all fears are learned. In order to get the victory over your fears, you must unlearn them by renewing your mind because your mind controls your brain (thoughts), and your thoughts generate energy. Discipline your thought life to listen to the Holy Spirit (John 14:26).

Let me help you out – there will always be fear when you come out of your comfort zone. When you dare to push yourself from where you are to where you want to be, you will feel some discomfort. Feel fear and do it anyway!

Joyce Meyer, teacher, preacher and author, said unapologetically, "Do it afraid." Nike, the kingdom of sneakers, said it best, "Just do it." Joshua 1:9 invokes a command, "Have I not commanded thee? Be strong and of good courage; be not afraid, neither be thou dismayed: for the Lord thy God is with thee whithersoever thou goest." Let's unpack this verse. I see six significant things.

Number one: *Command.* God has commanded us to deal with our fears. In other words, to take authority over our fears (2 Timothy 1:7). We must take dominion over our fears. It is not an option but a command. Instead of walking forward in faith, we are walking backwards in fear. The devil uses fear and worry as tools to take control of believer's lives. But the Bible tells us, "Submit to Him, resist the devil, and he will flee (James 4:7).

God assures us that, "He that dwelleth in the secret place of the most High shall abide under the shadow of the Almighty. I will say of the LORD, He is my refuge and my fortress: my God; in him will I trust. Surely he shall deliver thee from the snare of the fowler, and from the noisome pestilence. He shall cover thee with his feathers, and under his wings shalt thou trust: his truth shall be thy shield and buckler. Thou shall not be afraid for the terror by night; nor for the arrow that flieth by day; Nor for the pestilence that walketh in darkness; nor for the destruction that wasteth at noonday. A thousand shall fall at thy side, and ten thousand at thy right hand; but it shall not come nigh thee" (Psalm 91:1-7).

God promised that, "No weapon formed against you shall prosper, and every tongue that rises up against you in judgment shall be condemned" (Isaiah 54:17). If we abide in His Word, love Him with our whole heart, mind, body, soul, spirit, and love thy neighbor as thyself, He will give us the desires of our heart. When we walk in true fellowship with God, He commands a blessing upon us, and we will reap where we didn't plant. Stop trying to make things happen, and let God make things happen for you. He commands a blessing and not you. You don't have to fear, worry, stress-out or panic. Chill out, kick back, and let God do it for you.

God's prophet, Elijah, was in desperate need of provision due to the drought the land was experiencing. Because he was a covenant son, Elijah did not have to sort the problem out. God did it for him. He commanded a blessing to come. "Arise and go to Zarephath which belongs to Zidon, and there: I have commanded a widow woman there to provide for you" (1 Kings 17:9). Child of God, He knows your needs even before you ask Him. He knows you need a supernatural healing in your body. He knows you need a supernatural miracle. He knows you need a supernatural financial blessing. Trust God and lean not to your own understanding. Trust God's timing. Trust God when you can't trace Him.

Number two: *Be Strong and Courageous.* Life requires courage. God wants us to be strong and courageous not timid. Not fearful of the unknown or failure, but powerful enough to meet fear head on. Usually, we think brave people have no fear; but, the truth is they are intimate with fear. Joshua 1:9 says to be strong, but it is not talking about being physically fit. Neither is the text talking about joining a gym or lifting weights. It is talking about lifting the Word of God. Joshua 1:8 instruct us to, "Meditate on the word day and night, and let it not depart out of your mouth." God wants us to be strong and courageous.

I am reminded of the movie "The Wizard of Oz" where Bert Lahr played the cowardly lion. Lions are supposed to be the king of beasts. The cowardly lion believed that his fear made him inadequate. He did not understand that courage means acting in the face of fear. It takes courage to be your authentic self in this messed up world. It takes courage to stand up for God when non-believers surround you. It takes courage to be in this world, but not of this world. "For I am not ashamed of the gospel: for it is the power of God unto salvation to every one that believeth; first to the Jew then to the Gentile" (Romans 1:16). "God did not give us a spirit of fear; but of power, and of love, and of a sound mind" (2 Timothy 1:7). It's time to root up fear, worry, and distress.

On the other hand, it's time to bury some stuff. Bury the past, bury unforgiveness, and bury fear. It's time to live again. "Let the weak say that I am strong" (2 Corinthians 12:10). Where did fear come from? It came from the devil, the one who is trying to block you and stop you. The devil can only hold you hostage if you give him permission by backing up when he raises his ugly head. But greater strength is in you than all the devils in the world.

Courage is a choice to withstand the fiery darts of the devil. When knocked down, get back up again, shake the dust off your feet, and keep moving. Your choice is to fight the good fight of faith, to come out swinging instead of running, to keep on keeping on instead of quitting, to act with integrity rather than dishonestly, to move forward instead of backward, and to move out in faith instead of fear. You must choose to be unlike the cowardly lion that looks for courage outside of himself. God explicitly told us, "Fear not for I am with thee, be not dismayed; for I am thy God: I will strengthen thee; I will withhold thee with the right hand of my righteousness" (Isaiah 41:10).

Number three: *Don't Be Afraid.* The devil is not interested in how good or how bad you look. He doesn't care if your hair is short, long, straight, and curly, if you have a weave or if you're happy being nappy. The devil doesn't care if you live in a mansion or a shack. The devil doesn't care where you shop, whether it's Goodwill or Rodeo Drive. Nor does he care about your education or lack of education. What the devil wants is to put fear in your mind so that you won't live out your purpose. I want to take a moment to reiterate the true meaning of purpose. But before I do, I want to tell you what purpose is not. Purpose is not when someone prophesied or prophelied over your life. Purpose is not what someone said you would be good at. Purpose is not wanting to be someone other than yourself. Purpose is not what your parents want you to be. Purpose is none of those things. Listen to me carefully.

Purpose is discovering the gift God has put inside of you to use in service for others. Far too many people never fulfill the call of God on their lives simply because every time they try to go forward the devil uses fear to stop them. According to 1 John 4:18, "There's no fear in love; but perfect love casteth out fear: because fear hath torment. He that feareth is not made perfect in love." The devil wants to torment you through fear similar to all of the torment Jesus experienced when He was on His way to the cross; but, Jesus did not waiver. The devil tried to torment Him by saying, "Turn these stones into bread" (Matthew 4:3), but He did not waiver. We are no different when it comes to the devil's devices. Jesus told the devil, "Get behind me, Satan!" and you have to do the same thing (Matthew 16:23).

The devil sees you as a target to kill, steal from, and to destroy for his kingdom. But, "Death and life are in the power of the tongue" (Proverbs 18:21). You can talk the devil down by using faith-filled words. It's the Word of God that makes the devil flee. Pastor Sheryl Brady once said, "Every thought has an agenda. Your life will follow your thoughts." Listen, if we cultivate bad thoughts then bad thoughts begin to grow. Then, we water them with more negative thoughts. After that, we magnify them. Subsequently, they grow even bigger. Finally, they begin to reproduce like cancer cells eating away at us. Remember, whatever you feed will grow and whatever you starve will die.

Keep in mind that when you are a stand-up person for Jesus you will be targeted by the devil. Just know that he can't penetrate or infiltrate you when you are clothed in the whole armor of God according to Ephesians 6:11. Don't be high jacked by the devil. Don't fall prey to him. Keep the whole armor of God on. Don't take your armor off when you go to work. Don't take your armor off when you go on vacation or when you are around people with a form of Godliness but denying its power. "For as much then as Christ has suffered for us in the flesh, arm yourself likewise with the same mind" (1 Peter 4:1).

Les Brown (who I mentioned previously, is a motivational speaker and author) pointed out that, "Too many of us are not living our dreams, but living our fears." Psalm 27:1 tells me that, "The Lord is my light and my salvation; whom shall I fear? The Lord is the strength of my life; of whom shall I be afraid?" Your strength is not in your job. Your strength is not in your bank account. Your strength is not in your education. Your strength is not in your friend. God and God alone is the source of your strength.

A songwriter, once said: *"Lord, I will lift my eyes to the hills knowing my help comes from you. Your peace you give me in time of the storm. You are the source of my strength. You are the strength of my life. I lift my hands in total praise to you."* Amazing things happens when I praise God. I begin to feel something in the spiritual realm. I feel a fresh wind from the Holy Spirit. My ears are opened. My mind is tuned in to Him. My heart is fixed on Him. I am receptive to His voice. All of a sudden, I feel a certain release in my spirit. I don't feel helpless anymore. I don't feel fear anymore. I begin to feel His presence. I begin to clap my hands and stomp my feet. My problems seem to fade away. This makes me feel like everything is going to be alright. What am I doing? I am casting my cares on Him. I am honoring Him by giving Him my fears, doubts, worries, and concerns. He is bigger and stronger than my toughest problem.

Number four: *Don't be dismayed*. Have you ever felt like the more you try the worse things get? Have you ever worked on a project or an idea with little or no results? Is there a situation in your life right now that is causing you to be dismayed? Maybe it is causing you to lose your focus. Every day, we are faced with distractions, which cause us to detour from our focus. We are consumed by the requests of other people, and what disturbs me is that they should follow their own heart by asking the question, "What would Jesus do?"

Often, we allow other people's requests and predicaments to become ours. I am not saying that your friends should not ask you for advice, but they must learn to be dependent on God not on you. When we are consumed with other people's needs and desires, we become distracted, and distractions cause us to be dismayed. Subsequently, we become overwhelmed and burdened because we have too many irons in the fire, causing us to lose our focus. It was once said, "The sharper the focus is – the sharper you are." We must be focused, set priorities and keep the main thing the main thing. If we are going to do the significant things, we cannot get caught up in the insignificant things.

In this season of my life, I am learning how to say no. We are not indispensable. The show will go on with or without us. In this season of my life, I am only going to do what I am gifted and qualified to do. I am gifted to preach, pray, teach, and help others find their purpose so that they can find their destiny. Purpose is the motivator. Destiny is the end result. The main ingredients to reaching your full potential are: to stay focused in the midst of being dismayed, and to keep in mind that we are on this Earth for one reason – to make a difference.

Over and over, we find that God is saying to us (in one way or another), "Be not dismayed." If you are feeling dismayed, have a little talk with Jesus and tell Him all your troubles. Talk to Him before you get out of the bed, before you make your way to the bathroom, in the bathroom, while getting dressed, while driving to work, and on your break. Talk to God at the beginning of the day and at the end of the day. Make it personal. Speak His words back to Him. Tell him, "God, you said in Jeremiah 29:11, 'For I know the plans I have for you, to prosper you and give you an expected end.' God, I know what you put in my spirit. God, you said in Joel 2:25 that you would, 'Restore to me everything that the locust, cankerworm, caterpillar, and the palmerworm hath eaten.' God, you told me in 1 Corinthians 2:9 that, 'Eyes have not seen and ears have not heard the things you have prepared for me.' God, you said in Genesis 12:2 that you would make me a great nation, and make my name great. God, you said in Proverbs 10:22 that, 'The blessing of the Lord maketh rich and addeth no sorrow.' God, you said in Deuteronomy 28:2 that, 'The blessings will come on you and overtake you.'" God will never ask you to do something He has not equipped you to do. The shift starts with you. Move forward in the things God has called you to do. He said clearly in the Bible: "I will never leave you nor forsake you. I will be with you always even until the end of time" (Deuteronomy 31:6; Matthew 28:20). There is no secret to what God can do. Blessed be the name of the Lord!

Number five: *For the Lord **is***. The word *"is"* is a two-letter word that consists of a vowel and a constant. And although *"is"* begins many verses in the Bible, it is often overlooked despite its powerful and profound significance. It is the essence of the true meaning of God's Word. It makes God's Word clear, definite, and distinct. Do you think that it is alright to skip over or ignore the word *is*? Of course not, it is put there on purpose to awaken the reader to the depth, breadth and true meaning of the Word of God. The Lord *is* my shepherd. By not putting emphasis on each word in the verse especially the word *is,* both the reader and listener would think they can have salvation on their own terms. It is crucial that we don't pass over any of God's words too quickly.

The word *is* bears the framework, the building, and the backbone of God's prophetic words. 2 Timothy 3:16 says, "All scripture *is* given by inspiration of God, and is profitable for doctrine, for reproof, for correction, for instruction in righteousness." The Lord's words are flawless. He shields all that take refuge in Him.

We must slow down and read the Bible in its true context. If we don't, then we are deceiving ourselves, and deceiving the new converts we are trying to witness to. To read the Bible the way it is written, you must give up your own agenda. You have to dwell in the text and see the whole tapestry of the Bible from Genesis to Revelation. You must read the Bible as God's inspired and infallible written word. When you do, you will find that God speaks to you.

Number six: *Whithersoever thou goest I am with thee.* God knew that Joshua was going to have to deal with some stiff-necked people, so He told him to arm himself with the Word of God. God told Joshua to meditate on the Word day and night, to be strong, to be courageous, and to not be afraid or dismayed. He told Joshua that just like He was with Moses, He would be with him. He promised not to forsake him, leave him, or give up on him. That lets me know that God is someone I can count on, and someone that I can trust in. Someone I can rely on. Someone I can put my confidence and hope in during troubled times.

"Trust in the Lord with all thine heart; lean not to your own understanding" (Proverbs 3:5). I am so glad that God did not say to put your trust in men and women because they will fail you almost all the time. He said trust in Him and He will be with you whithersoever you go. God will be with you through the tough times. God will hold you in the hollow of His hands. If you're struggling today: First, cry out to Jesus. "When the righteous cry out for help, the Lord hears and delivers them from all of their troubles" (Psalm 34:17). Second, sing praises to God. Acts 16:25 says that when Paul and Silas were in prison they prayed and sang praises unto God. God said, "I am with you whithersoever thou goest" (Joshua 1:9). Now, these words blessed my heart, mind, and soul. How encouraging it is to know that whithersoever I go He is with me. I take comfort in the magnitude of God's omniscience.

I take comfort in knowing that He restores my soul. I take comfort in knowing that the battle is not mine, but His. I take comfort in knowing that He has a plan for my life. A plan that will prosper me and give me an expected end (Jeremiah 29:11). That gives me a burst of new energy. His plan is my purpose. Remember, you are not waiting on your purpose; your purpose is waiting on you. Your purpose was in you before you were formed in your mother's womb (Jeremiah 1:5).

The gift that God has gifted you with is in your genetic make-up. It is in your DNA, your RNA, your fingerprints, your chromosomes, and your genes. But what happens is we are so busy looking at someone else's purpose, and trying to be like them. As a result, we are blinded and cannot see our own purpose. My question is simple. While you are trying to be like someone else, who's going to be you? Live your own purpose! Then, your life will have meaning and fulfillment. What's more, you can face each morning with new energy and renewed enthusiasm. Your happy Friday will be happy Monday, happy Tuesday, happy Wednesday, and happy Thursday. Furthermore, rainy days will become your best friend.

God will be with you wherever you go. You are not on this journey alone. God is our burden-bearer, our bridge over troubled water, our midnight rider, our sounding board and our company keeper. If you need to vent, call on the great name of Jesus. Isaiah 26:3 says, "Thou will keep him in perfect peace, whose mind is stayed on thee: because he trusteth in thee." God will be with you every step you take. He is watching over you to perform His word concerning your life. God has a master plan for each one of us, but it is up to us to surrender to His will. It's important to know that you can have assurance in God's plan. Let Him work out His purpose for your life.

Too many of us live in constant fear because in the past many negative and hurtful things have happened to us, leaving us wondering, "Where is God? Why hasn't He answered my prayers? Why would a loving, just God allow me to suffer?" But, "Be not dismayed, if we suffer with him, we will reign with him: if we deny him, he also will deny us" (2 Timothy 2:12). We must be like Jesus in the Garden of Gethsemane when He declared, "Nevertheless, not my will but thine will be done" (Luke 22:42).

God is not sitting in Heaven wondering who you are in Christ. He knows your name. He knows the number of hairs on your head. He knows your address. He knows you inside and out; the good, the bad, and the ugly. He is trying to awaken the giant that's in you. He's not sitting in Heaven wondering how to find a fit for your life. He's not trying to work it out; He's already figured it out. 1 Peter 5:9 says, "The God of all grace, who called us unto his eternal glory by Christ Jesus, after ye have suffered a while, make you perfect, stablish, strength and settle you." Sometimes, it seems the more you try, the worse things get. Sometimes, it seems that things are not going the way you want them to go. Sometimes, God allows suffering for the perfecting of the saints. But be ye confident, He will never leave you nor forsake you. God will not tell you all of the details, but rest assured He will be with you. When God told Abraham to get out of his country from among his kinfolks, he didn't give him all of the pieces to the puzzle, but he did tell him that He would be with him wherever he goes. King David, a man after God's own heart, testified, "I once was young and now I am old, yet I have never seen the righteous forsaken nor his seed begging bread" (Psalm 37:25).

Recall that in Joshua 1 we saw God encouraging Joshua in the faith. The Lord spoke to Joshua and said, "Moses my servant is dead. Get ready! Cross the Jordan River! Lead these people into the land, which I am ready to hand over to them. I am handing over to you every place you set foot, as I promised Moses" (Joshua 1:2-3). Then God reassured Joshua that he didn't need to worry because He would not abandon him. God promised that He would be there before Joshua got there. He would be there when the sun rises and when the sunsets. He would guide the people with a cloud by day and a pillar of fire by night, and He would remove every stumbling block, roadblock, and pothole that got in the way.

Don't look to the right nor to the left. He will make the crooked places straight. Don't be fearful of what you feel, hear or see along the way. Don't be dismayed or afraid; just keep walking by faith and not by sight. Psalm 119:105 says, "Thy word is a lamp to my feet and a light unto my path."

I want you to know that God is arranging and rearranging things in your life. Everything will work together for His glory. Your end was already set before you began. In other words, God is saying: "I got this. I am with you wherever you go." When I look back over my life, I can see God's hands. When I am weak, His strength is made perfect. When I am fearful, He is fearless. When I am afraid, He is unafraid. When I am discouraged, He encourages me. When I am lonely, He comforts me. When I am dismayed, He is cool, calm and collected.

DECLARATION OF OWNERSHIP (XII)

THE POWER OF I AM
For God has not given us a spirit of fear;
but of power and of love, and of a sound mind.
2 Timothy 1:7

I AM NOT A WORRYWART
Therefore, I say unto you, take no thought for your
life, what ye shall eat, or what ye shall drink;
Nor yet for your body, what ye shall put on.
Is not the life more than meat and the body than
raiment?
Matthew 6:25

I AM NOT A WHINER
Peace I leave with you, my peace I give unto you:
not as the world giveth, give I unto you. Let not
your heart be troubled, neither let it be afraid.
John 14:27

I AM NOT A COMPLAINER
Say to them that are of a fearful heart, be strong,
fear not: behold, your God will come with a recompense; he
will come and save you.
Isaiah 35:4

I AM NOT STRESSING
Peace I leave with you, my peace I give unto you:
not as the world giveth, give I unto you. Let not
your hearts be troubled, neither let it be afraid.
John 14:27

I AM NOT AFRAID
Be strong and of a good courage,
fear not, nor be afraid of them: for the Lord thy
God, he it is that doth go with thee;
he will not fail thee, nor forsake thee.
Deuteronomy 31:6

I AM NOT FEARFUL

The angel of the Lord encampeth round about them that fear him and delivereth them. O taste and see that the Lord is good: blessed is the man that trusteth in him.
Psalm 34:7-8

CHAPTER 14
It's an Inside Job

*The soul of a sluggard desireth, and hath nothing:
but the soul of the diligent shall be made fat.*
Proverbs 13:4

Discipline is one of the most hated terms of our times – right along with patience and determination. But have you noticed how often it comes up in the testimonies of those who win? No athlete completes the training of a race without it. No human body is kept fit without it. If you want to put a stop to disorder and replace excuses with vigorous determination, you need discipline.

My life's purpose, which I live by every day, is to help someone else find theirs; to help others achieve their highest potential and live their best lives by encouraging them that all things are possible. I am passionate about helping others to be all that they have dreamed about, and all that is screaming inside of them trying to get out.

I want to admonish you to follow through no matter what the circumstances. I want you to be all that you desire to be, fulfill your destiny, and believe that there is greatness inside of you. I want you to hear my heart. The questions I will pose to you next are thought provoking. What bothers you the most? What captivates your thoughts? What holds your interest? What matters to you? We find many reasons for deferring action on important tasks. For instance, I have been busy with other tasks that have prevented me from finishing this book. In the interim, I have completed many other tasks of lesser importance. The unfinished task nags me and spoils the joy I should find in accomplishments. Our delaying and indecision may result in discouragement, irritation, and self-disappointment.

Some challenges may be so difficult that they seem overpowering. For example: I plan to eat healthier. I'll read the Bible through in one year. I'll listen more and talk less. How easy it is to defer challenging tasks. A lack of willpower, self-discipline and determination delay us. We welcome interruptions. Many of us await flashes of inspiration to stir us up.

I was watching the PGA Championship, and there were plenty of moments when you thought Pro Golfer, Rory McIlroy, wouldn't win his fourth major championship, for the second time in a row, at the age of twenty-five. But, the whole tournament changed on Thursday when Rory got to the hole that gave us one of his weirdest swings. An over-hooked three-wood went out of bounds and led to a double-bogey, his only of the tournament. Rory pulled the same club from 280 yards that he had on Sunday, hit it to 12-feet rolling in the eagle putt, and started the inevitable march to victory. I see it as sheer determination and discipline when you draw on your reserves and your desire to win.

As you may recall from Chapter 12, I was bullied when I was in grade school. That experience left me with a mental scar that I think about from time to time. But, it also left me with sheer determination, and discipline to change how I viewed myself on the inside no matter what I had experienced in grade school. Nowadays, I stick my chest out, square my shoulders, lift my head up, and say, "Look at me now!" I am living a blessed life. I like living this kind of life. I want to share with you four priceless pointers that have added value to my life.

Number one: *Change the way you think about yourself.* (Philippians 4:8). Your mind must be born again. It's an inside job. Trading in the old for the new. Give yourself an extensive brainwashing, and strip off negative thoughts that hold your mind in captivity. This will allow you to have a renewed way of thinking. Exchange your words by gaining full control of what's going on in your mind. This is easier said than done. We need to recognize change as a paradigm shift: new, innovative ideas for old, outdated ideas. Change is the only constant in life. When we change, we grow.

Number two: *No goal is out of reach* (Philippians 4:13). You can do whatever you believe you can do even if it seems like all of the odds are against you. To achieve your goals, stay focused on your objectives, working diligently through your adversities, obstacles, and challenges. You can make your mark in life when you trade in the insignificant, unproductive things for the significant, productive things.

Number three: *How do you see yourself?* Your identity is very important. The Bible says in 1 Peter 2:9, "You are a chosen generation, a royal priesthood, and a holy nation." Furthermore, you are fearfully and wonderfully made (Psalm 139:14). When you lay hold of what's on the inside of you, it will not be long before it is revealed on the outside of you. Your thoughts are an inside job, so unshackle your mind. Delusional thinking is a kind of prison that restricts you from your personal desires. Our job is to free ourselves from prison – the prison of fear, the prison of failure, the prison of doubt, the prison of distrust, and the prison of offenses.

True freedom is when we liberate the liberator. The problem is that we have built a wall to protect ourselves from those who dare to invade our nuisances, such as our right to fear, fuss, and fret. We are suspicious of everything and everybody. Once we recognize this pattern of behavior and take action, we will stop hoarding yesterday's junk. We can't be blindsided by yesterday's offenses, failures, or transgressions. Author, Louise Smith wrote: "You can't reach for anything new if your hands are still full of yesterday's junk."

Put your determination where your desires are. The difference between hoping and wishing is significant. A wish is a desire for something that seems unattainable. But, nothing is impossible with God. Hope is a desire with expectation of attainment. Hope with confidence. This is the confidence I have in Him. Hope cherishes a desire with anticipation. Jesus said, "Ask, seek, knock, and the door shall be opened" (Matthew 7:7). Well, this is good news because all you have to do is step inside the open door and reap the benefits. Hope breed's faith. "Faith is the substance of things hoped for and the evidence of things not seen" (Hebrews 11:1). I like to put it like this: Faith is stepping out from where you are to where you want to go (hopefully to the next level). Can I get an Amen? Put your faith into action – action requires energy. Make faith your steering wheel that directs your path.

A faithful determination generates grace, and "God's grace is sufficient" (2 Corinthians 12:9). It's the everyday crap that constipates the mind. When you find, yourself drifting down the wrong road, maybe you need to sound the alarm and make a U-turn. Matthew 7:13-14 says, "Enter through the narrow gate. For wide is the gate and broad is the road that leads to destruction, and many enter through it." I like the way the Message Bible puts it: "Don't look for shortcuts to

God. The market is flooded with surefire, easygoing formulas for a successful life that can be practiced in your spare time. Don't fall for that stuff, even though crowds of people do. The way to life – to God! – is vigorous and requires total attention." In other words, don't fall for the okie dokie.

Number four: *Who are you?* Have you ever thought about who you are? What you stand for? I am not talking about your roles or social identities. You can be a friend, brother, sister, employee, boyfriend, girlfriend, spouse, mother, father, son, or daughter, all at the same time, but those are just aspects of you. They don't represent the total you. Your inner self is who you are on the inside. Today, most of us are accustomed to wearing masks at carnivals, festivals, and children's parties. Often, masks are survival tools that we wear to cover up the truth of how we really feel. We wear masks to protect ourselves from pain, suffering, hurt, physical and emotional turmoil.

Let me give you an example from my own life. I grew up in a small, southern town with many role expectations and cultural conditions. One of those expectations was that women should not wear pants to church. I didn't see any good reason why I shouldn't wear pants if I wanted to; but, in order to fit in and be viewed as a lady, I conformed. Nowadays, I wear what I want when I want. I wear what I feel – suit, dress, pants, hat, gloves, stockings or no stockings. Today, pants are a major part of my wardrobe. My hope for you is that you allow your inner self to emerge by revealing the real you. Stop pretending that you are something you are not. It is so much easier to be yourself without wearing a Halloween mask. Know and love yourself for being the person God created you to be. He created you in His image. Oprah Winfrey once said: "Don't get confused between what people say you are and who you know you are."

The limiting, false beliefs we hold about ourselves are like powerful swords that can cut through our confidence, self-worth, and self-image just as a razorblade cuts through the flesh. Apply God's Word to enrich your faith and grow in spiritual maturity. Use it as your double-edged sword. "For the word of God is quick and powerful, and sharper than any two-edged sword, piercing even to the dividing asunder of soul and spirit and of the joints and marrow; and is a discerner of the thoughts and intents of the heart" (Hebrews 4:12). Let God's Word deepen your confidence, self-worth, and self-image. When you change what you believe about yourself and your abilities, you unleash your inner self. A joyful, energetic, confident, and purposeful life is not an option. Can you imagine how your life would change if you disciplined your thoughts? It's an inside job. Trade in the old for the new!

DECLARATION OF OWNERSHIP (XIII)

THE POWER OF I AM
*He becometh poor that dealeth with a slack
hand: but the hand of the diligent maketh rich.*
Proverbs 10:4

I AM A FINISHER
*The hand of diligent shall bear rule:
but the slothful shall be under tribute.*
Proverbs 12:24

I AM PROFICIENT
*Seest thou a man diligent in his business? He shall
stand before kings; he shall not stand before men.*
Proverbs 22:29

I AM PERSISTENT
*He that diligently seeketh good procureth favour
but he that seeketh mischief, it shall come unto him.*
Proverbs 11:27

I AM A HUMAN "ANT"
*Go to the ant, thou sluggard;
consider her ways, and be wise:
Which having no guide, overseer, or ruler, provideth
her meat in the summer, and gathereth her food in the harvest.
How long wilt thou sleep, O sluggard?
When wilt thou arise out of thy sleep?*
Proverbs 6:6-9

I AM WISE
*He that tilleth his land shall be satisfied with bread:
but he that followeth vain persons is void of understanding.*
Proverbs 12:11

I AM BLESSED
*The blessing of the LORD, it maketh
rich and he addeth no sorrow with it.*
Proverbs 10:2

CHAPTER 15
Dismiss Distractions

*Let thine eyes look right on, and let
thine eyelids look straight before thee.*
Proverbs 4:25

There is one specific area in my life I struggle with and it is all of the endless distractions. I become easily distracted by irrelevant sounds, smells, noise, clatter, and commotion. One of my biggest challenges is staying focused and maximizing the moment. It's a never-ending battle that I war with daily. It can be difficult to avoid distractions while preparing for a project. If you struggle with distractions like I do, try some focusing techniques. First, identify the distractions that are keeping you from focusing. Some of these distractions could be: social media, television, and your cell phone. Turn off those enticing gadgets. By doing so, you will complete tasks more quickly and efficiently. Proper preparation defeats distractions. Distractions can lead us astray, causing us to forgo our objective; subsequently leading to failure to achieve our goals.

Distractions were what happened to the ten bridesmaids in Matthew 25:1-13, but five of them were wise and five of them were foolish. The foolish ones took their lamps but did not take any oil with them. The wise ones however, took oil in jars along with their lamps. The bridegroom (Jesus) was long-time in coming, and they all became drowsy and fell asleep. At midnight, the cry rang out: "Here's the bridegroom come out and meet him." Then, all the virgins woke up and trimmed their lamps. The foolish ones said to the wise, "Give us some of your oil. Our lamps are going out." "No," the wise virgins replied, "There may not be enough for both of us. Instead, go to those who sell oil and buy some for yourselves." But while they were on their way to buy the oil, the bridegroom arrived. The virgins who were ready went in with Him to the wedding banquet, and the door was shut behind them. The others came later. "Lord, Lord," they said, "open the door for us." But He replied, "Truly I tell you I don't know you." Therefore, keep watch, because you do not know the day or the hour."

How many needless times have we missed an opportunity because we were not prepared? We are not failures; we simply are not wise with our time. We have been given great opportunities, but for some reason we have failed to pursue them. The parable was not written to praise virginity. Neither does the parable criticize these virgins for sleeping. They all slept. Nor does the parable show favoritism. All of the virgins had lamps. The parable was written for us to value preparedness. I read an article about distractions and how to unclutter your mind. The article indicated that sometimes there are things on your mind that you have no control over. These may be hurtful things from your past or worries about the future. Either way, you need to let go of these burdensome thoughts and feelings and move on. If you can't do anything about them, then there is no benefit to holding on to them.

You can't change the past, but you can change your future right now. Think hard about what you want to do for the rest of your life. And don't cut off a thought by saying, "I am too old," "I am no longer capable," or "I am unworthy." Remember, "Death and life are in the power of the tongue" (Proverbs 18:21). You just have to take the first step toward achieving your dream. Start today by making a declaration. The Bible says, "If you declare a thing it will be established for you" (Job 22:28). "Through faith, we understand that the world was framed by the word of God, so that things which are seen were not made of things which do appear" (Hebrews

11:3). Words kill. Words also give life. It is time to shift the tide of our lives. It is time to quit asking our Heavenly Father to do something He already did at the cross. If you are allowing distractions to invade your daily schedule, here are some things to think about.

Number one: *Prepare for Distractions. Doing things over and over without proper preparation is insanity.* Let's look at what goes into preparation. When you get ready to take a trip or vacation, first you decide where you want to go. You decide the best time to travel. You book your flight in advance. You make a choice of hotels and your duration of stay. Jesus said in John 14:3, "And if I go and prepare a place for you, I will come again, and receive you unto myself; that where I am, there ye may be also." The Parable of the Ten Virgins does suggest that five of the virgins were not prepared, and when you are unprepared its likely due to distractions. Unlike those virgins, Noah (who walked faithfully with God) prepared an Ark for his family and told the neighboring people it was going to rain. Afterward, God closed the door, and those who did not board the Ark, because their minds were muddled with distractions, perished. I don't know about you, but when I break down each of the tasks given to Noah, it sounds nearly impossible. But, the Bible says, "With other people this is impossible, but with God all things are possible" (Matthew 19:26).

Some days, you are going to feel overwhelmed with everything you have left to do. Yet, bear in mind that God has appointed and anointed you for such a time as this. God can use the impossible to accomplish the possible. God has a history of asking unlikely people to do big things, and then working through them to complete the task. "Be anxious for nothing, but in everything by prayer and supplication with thanksgiving let your request be known unto God" (Philippians 4:6). There's an adage that rings true today: "Rome was not built in a day." God knows what you have left to do. When life has you feeling overwhelmed, Jesus said in Matthew 11:28, "Come unto me, all ye who are labour and are heavy laden, I will give you rest." So, when you become weary and feel like giving up, don't! Listen, everybody is going through something whether it is physical, emotional, financial, or spiritual. When you are going through a crisis, you don't have to go through it alone. Understand that God is close to the broken-hearted. It's in the crisis that the devil wants you to surrender. Pain comes when we resist surrendering. Submit yourselves therefore to God. Resist the devil, and he will flee from you (James 4:7).

Number two: *Fight Discouragement.*
Discouragement is a powerful tool the devil uses as a stronghold to choke out our relationship with God. Moses, "The Great Deliverer," told the people of Israel what the Lord said, but they refused to listen to him anymore. They had become too discouraged by the brutality of their slavery. Discouragement is a psychological disease. No one is exempt, even me. You might be discouraged at this very moment. Frustration causes discouragement. A deeper look at Moses' story provides the perfect example.

God told Moses to speak to a rock, promising to make water flow in the desert again. But, instead of speaking to the rock, Moses struck it. Because of that one thing, God told Moses that He would no longer be permitted to bring the people into The Promised Land. The people of Israel were not the easiest people in the world to minister to. They criticized Moses, they judged him, and they resisted him. They did not like the way Moses led them or fed them. The Israelites wanted to go back to Egypt to live in bondage. They wanted to eat leeks, onions, and garlic. Have you ever done something for someone and they were ungrateful and unappreciative? Well, this was what Moses had to put up with. The Israelites did not like the manna that came from Heaven. I suppose that kind of reaction would have caused anybody to go off. Discouragement visits all of us.

Many times, one has to hit rock bottom before finding a firm foundation. It is when we have lost our way and all hope that we find the blessed hope. The Bible says, "Look unto the hills which comes your help. Your help comes from the Lord which made the heaven and earth" (Psalm 121:1-2). Jesus is the author and the finisher of our faith, where we find amazing grace, unmerited mercy, and supernatural favor. I don't know about you, but He has brought me out of a horrible pit, out of the miry clay, set me on a rock, and established my goings (Psalm 40:2-3). The Lord has put a running in my feet, a clapping in my hands, and a "Hallelujah! Thank you, Jesus, for all You have done for me," in my mouth.

Distractions are the death of dreams. But once you refocus, then you begin to get back on track. You begin to release energy that has been in reserve. There's something inside of you so strong that is waiting to be released. Too many of us have suppressed our dreams. We have framed our dreams and hung them on a wall to be admired by family and friends. We have lost the fire that used to invigorate our dreams. We must find it again and harness it.

Number three: *Push Past Doubt.* Sometimes, I doubt how to start a project. I find myself uncertain about what topic to begin with first. Other times, I doubt my instincts. But what I am learning is that the only "wrong" choice is not making one. That's not to say that we'll always create the outcomes we visualize, but maybe that isn't the point. Maybe the point is to learn to be less afraid of leaping, knowing that if I stay in the nest indefinitely there won't be room to spread my wings. This is something I have been thinking about a lot lately as I stretch outside of my comfort zone with public preaching. As a loner, this can be daunting, let alone crowds of people staring at me and sizing me up while I talk passionately about something I love. Realize that your success or failure depends on you. Dismiss distractions. Don't find an excuse find a way. "I can do all things through Jesus Christ who strengthens me" (Philippians 4:13).

DECLARATION OF OWNERSHIP (XIV)

THE POWER OF I AM
*And this I speak for your own profit;
not that I may cast a snare upon you,
but for that which is comely, and that ye
may attend upon the Lord without distraction.*
1 Corinthians 7:35

I AM CASTING MY CARES ON HIM
And the cares of this world, and the deceitfulness of riches, and the lusts of other things entering in, choke the word, and it becometh unfruitful.
Mark 4:19

I AM SOWING INTO GOOD GROUND
And some fell on thorns; and the thorns sprang up with it, and choked it.
Luke 8:7

I AM ABLE TO BEAR IT
There hath no temptation taken you but such as is common to man: but God is faithful, who will not suffer you to be tempted above that ye are able; but will with the temptation also make a way to escape, that ye may be able to bear it.
1 Corinthians 10:13

I AM RESTORING MY MIND
And be not conformed to this world: but be ye transformed by the renewing of your mind, that ye may prove what is good, and acceptable, and perfect, will of God.
Romans 12:2

I AM A LOVER OF GOD
If any man love the world, the love of the Father is not in him.
1 John 2:15

I AM LOOKING UP
Look unto me, and be ye saved, all the ends of the earth: for I am God, and there is none else.
Isaiah 45:22

CHAPTER 16
From This Day Forward
Watch and stand fast in the faith be strong, be brave.
1 Corinthians 16:13

How do we move from where we are to where we want to go? How do we pull out the greatness that's inside of us? How do we move forward when everything seems hopeless? This only happens when there is a change in your thinking. It is necessary that we look beyond limitations, obstacles, and adversity. Thinking starts the process of your destiny. Thinking starts the beginning of a remarkable journey. Philippians 4:8 tells us, "Think on things that are true, honest, just, pure, lovely, and things of a good report." Just think about how lovely it's going to be when the day comes that you finally reach some goals. But, thinking alone is not enough. Only movement obtains goals.

Almost everyone in the Bible had to move into his or her destiny. Move beyond the situation no matter how hard the problem is. When you are working out, you don't just stand there and do nothing, you walk, you run, you jog, you jump, and you dance. You move! The devil wants you to stand still and do nothing. The devil is a liar. You are a child of The Most High God. You are highly favored of the Lord. Blessed are you among women (Luke 1:28). You are to run the race and in the race, you don't stand still.

There are gratifying moments in our lives that change the course of our destiny. Our Lord and Savior, Jesus Christ, has bestowed things upon us. It has been pre-decided that we will have a favorable outcome. A college education is a pathway to success and a better life. Money and hard work can buy you many things.

However, one day of favor can save you a lifetime of labor.

Favor is likened unto grace. Favor is likened unto mercy. Favor is likened unto kindness. I just believe God favors me. I believe that I have preferential treatment with God. I believe God is blessing me right now! Your day is coming, so get your dancing shoes on. Don't wait until the battle is over. It's time to party! In Corinthians 16:13, the Apostle Paul gave a command, but it goes further. There are four imperatives in this verse.

Number one: *Watch.* What does it mean to watch? The word watch means to lookout, be sober, and be vigilant. As Christians, we should keep an eye on the world around us, and more importantly pay attention to our condition. The King James Version of 1 Corinthians 10:13 says, "There hath no temptation taken you but such as is common to man: but God is faithful, who will not suffer you to be tempted above that ye are able; but will with the temptation also make a way to escape, that ye may be able to bear it." I like the way the Message Bible puts it "No test or temptation that comes your way is beyond the course of what others had to face. All you need to remember is that God will never let you down; he'll never let you be pushed past your limit; he'll always be there to help you come through it."

Now, let's examine the text. Notice what it did not say. It did not say that tests or temptations would not come. They're going to come. But, you must get a handle on them because you have an adversary to fight (Ephesians 6:12). Some people feel that the only way to get a handle on temptation successfully is to yield to it. But, if you are weak in an area, you have to deal with that weakness in a spiritual manner. In other words, you have to come out swinging your double-edged sword, and that double-edged sword is the Word of God (Hebrews 4:12).

A student asked his teacher, "How do you resist temptation?" The teacher responded, "I always have a little talk with the devil." As for me, I just simply say, "Get behind me, Satan." When you speak the Word of God, the devil will flee from you (James 4:7). Our greatest temptation happens when we let our guard down. Temptation never goes on vacation. Most of us get a day or two off from work and we go on vacation. But, there is no such thing as a spiritual day off. The devil is on his job 24/7. He never takes a day off. Temptation often comes when we're off duty. For instance, when you are in a spiritual slump, when you let your guard down, when you are not "worded and prayed up," when you are not in fellowship with God or other believers, then you become an easy target for the devil to sift you as wheat (Luke 22:31).

What is temptation? Temptation means to entice, tempt, and to draw. Temptation is nothing new. Temptation is not going away. For example, just because you want to stop drinking alcohol, smoking cigarettes, or using illegal drugs doesn't mean they're going to close all of the liquor stores, smoke shops, or marijuana dispensaries. Let me be clear, the Bible does not forbid people to drink; however, the Bible does say, "Don't be drunk with wine" (Ephesians 5:18). Excessive drinking and drug use can lead to an addiction and increased risk of health concerns.

Temptation is as old as Adam and Eve in The Garden of Eden. I thought to myself, "What would have happened if Adam and Eve would have recited the

Word of God to the devil?" We must watch the things we say and do. It's our duty to mankind. We don't want to cause others to stumble. Don't become a stumbling block to the weak (1 Corinthians 8:9). To truly follow Christ means we no longer walk in darkness, but instead we walk in His light.

I believe each Christian should read and reread the book of Proverbs. It has loads of wisdom on how to tame the tongue. The same tongue that speaks healing can speak hurt. The familiar saying, "Sticks and stones may break my bones, but words will never hurt me" is one of the biggest lies that are ever been told. Also, we must watch our associations. In other words, watch people and your connection with them. Love them, but love God more and let Him be your guiding light.

Let's look at the relationship in the Old Testament between David, the sheepherder, and Saul, Israel's first king. David was loyal and served Saul faithfully; and, because of David's wisdom and bravery, King Saul entrusted him to do many things. David went wherever Saul sent him. David behaved himself wisely and the people (including Saul's servants) accepted him even though he was young. Whoever God calls, he qualifies.

One day, on the way back from the slaughter of Goliath, "The Champion of the Philistines," the women of the city of Israel were outside dancing, singing, and waiting to meet King Saul. They had musical instruments, and they were very joyful because their enemy, the Philistines, had been killed. The Israelites cheerfully chanted, "Saul has killed thousands, but David has killed tens of thousands" (1 Samuel 18:7). Suddenly, Saul felt a rage of jealousy. From that time on, Saul hated David and kept an eye on him wherever he went. Has someone hated you and all you wanted was the best for them?

In the past, King Saul disobeyed God and as result an evil spirit would sometimes trouble him. David, a skilled musician, would play his harp to soothe Saul during those times. The day after the Israelites sang their songs, the evil spirit came upon Saul and as usual, David played his harp for King Saul to comfort him. As David beautifully played the harp, King Saul threw a javelin twice at David, but God stayed the hand of death. That's why people call Jesus "An On-Time God." The Lord was with David, and He is with you! Saul hated David because of the favor on David's life. How can you love God who you have never seen and hate your brother and sister who you see every day (1 John 4:20)? By the way, hating is a sin. "Fret not thyself because of evildoers, neither be thou envious against the workers of iniquity. For they shall soon be cut down like grass, and wither as the green herb" (Psalm 37:1-2). You might be in a hard place right now, but God is such a God that He can turn your hard place around in the blink of an eye.

Number two: *Stand fast in faith.* What does it mean to stand fast in faith? To stand fast in faith means to be stationary, anchored, and convicted in your beliefs. When I am working out on the stationary bike, the bike is moving, but it never leaves the spot where it is sitting. It is in a fixed position. You can pedal as fast as you can go, and it will not move. You can stand up or sit down and it won't move. You can slow it down or speed it up and it won't move. It is fixed upon its foundation.

A songwriter once wrote: *"Though the storms keep on raging in my life, and sometimes it's hard to tell the night from day. Still that hope that lies within is reassured as I keep my eyes upon the distant shore; I know He'll lead me safely to that blessed place He has prepared. But if the storms don't cease, and if the winds keep on blowing in my life, my soul has been anchored in the Lord."*

Jesus is anchored to His Father. He is sitting in Heaven on the right-hand side of the Father. He is interceding on our behalf. He is working behind the scenes. Do you not know that God can take the impossible or the insignificant and remold, remake, and refurbish what seemed to be a hopeless situation? Stand fast in your faith; anchored in the Word of God against all odds. "There is a way which seemeth right unto a man, but the end thereof are the ways of death" (Proverbs 14:12).

Number three: *Be courageous.* What does it mean to be courageous in your beliefs no matter how much social media, society, or the "new norm movement" tries to influence, persuade, or convince you? The book of Ruth contains an interesting story about a Moabite woman who was redeemed into a Hebrew family. Ruth, an unlikely stranger, was used to fulfill God's plan and leave a legacy. The book of Ruth demonstrates God's providence at work in the life of an individual, and it exalts family loyalty. It shows how a Gentile became part of the Davidic lineage (Ruth 4:17-21). Ruth is cited in the genealogy of Christ in Matthew 1:5. Ruth's story is a legacy for all to glean from and admire.

What are you doing to leave a legacy for the next generation? You can choose what people will remember about you. What ideas do you have that are lying dormant? Small steps lead to big dividends. Just like Ruth, you might feel like an outsider who has lost what you had because of some unfortunate incident. You might feel lost in a great big world, but God has not forgotten about you. The enemy wants you to think that it's all over and done with, and that you are history. I come to tell somebody, "Don't panic. It's not over until God says it over!"

There are those of you who over the past years have set out with a commitment in mind, and now it looks as if God nailed the windows shut and slammed the door in your face. You have lost your faith in God. You feel like life has dealt you a bad hand because of some catastrophe. Perhaps there is something unpleasant going on in your family, maybe a sickness or a disease that has attached itself to you or a loved one, or possibly a financial hardship. Listen don't quit. Don't give up. Troubles don't last always. You will get through this. You are stronger than you think you are. It's only a test to make you stronger and wiser. You are built to outlast your troubles. I don't care how bad it looks; you are coming out of this. And when it's all said and done, you won't look like what you have been through.

God is going to break down the high places, and make the crooked places – things that you thought were unreachable, unattainable, unachievable, and untouchable – straight. He's going to give you double for your trouble. Start calling those things that are not as if they were (Romans 4:17). Speak boldly over your life. Start decreeing and declaring things over your life. Do you know who you are? You are not what people say about you, you are what the Bible says about you. You are delivered, forgiven and set free. You are a child of The Most High God. Act like it, walk like it, and most of all talk like it. God tells me who I am and what I can have. I shall have everything the Bible says I can have. I can do what the Bible says I can do. His Word says, "I can do all things through Christ who strengthens me" (Philippians 4:13). His Word says, "I once was young now I am old, but I have never seen the righteous forsaken nor his seed begging bread (Psalm 37:25). His Word says, "Many are the afflictions of the righteous, but God delivers them out of them all" (Psalm 34:19). His Word says, "I am the head and not the tail" (Deuteronomy 28:13). Get that depressed look off your face. Lift your head up and walk in authority. You talk the talk – start walking it! Walk out your purpose and don't let anything or anyone get in the way of the things you desire. Now is the appointed time. What are you waiting for? A parked car can't move. Start moving toward the desires of your heart. Don't wait another hour, another day, another week or another year.

"Today, if you hear the Word of God harden not your heart" (Hebrews 3:15). You don't have all the time in the world. Your season starts right now. Don't wait to make a New Year's resolution that you probably won't keep. I am weary of people who make excuses for not following through on their dreams. Some people think that just saying what they want to do with their life is as good as doing it. Not so! This is called wishful thinking. Far too many people make excuses about what they want to achieve.

Talking about your desires and dreams is useless without action. Talk is cheap, always has been and always will be. If you want a better life, you must do something other than just talk about it. Whatever you sow is what you will reap. If you sow procrastination, laziness, and wishful thinking, that is exactly what you are going to reap. I rebuke every lazy spirit of procrastination. I rebuke slothfulness. Listen, you must put your hands to the plow if you want a harvest. Take courage and break up the fallow ground if you want a bumper crop.

Number four: *Be strong.* What does strong mean? Strong means to increase in vigor, to be strengthened, and to increase in faith. Faith is a doorway to abundance. It's the key to unlimited treasure. Search the scriptures that speak to your weaknesses then stand on the promises of God. Be resilient no matter the odds. If someone tries to discourage you from living out your purpose, don't listen to them, turn a deaf ear. Only listen to the well-wishers and not the naysayers. What God has instilled in you is far greater than any negative propaganda. Focus on your possibilities and not your problems. God is bigger than any of our wants and needs, and stronger than our toughest problem. Therefore, be strong, steadfast, unmovable, and always abounding in the work of the Lord because your labor is not in vain (1 Corinthians 15:58).

DECLARATION OF OWNERSHIP (XV)

THE POWER OF I AM
I have set the Lord always before me:
because he is at my right hand,
I shall not be moved.
Psalm 16:8

I AM COURAGEOUS
The wicked flee when no man pursueth:
but the righteous are bold as a lion.
Proverbs 28:1

I AM ENDUED WITH POWER
But ye shall receive power, after that the Holy Ghost
is come upon you: and ye shall be witnesses unto
me both in Jerusalem, and in all Judea, and Samaria,
and unto the uttermost part of the earth.
Acts 1:8

I AM SELF-ASSURED
And now, Lord, behold their threatenings:
And grant unto thy servants, that with
all boldness they speak thy word.
Acts 4:29

I AM CONFIDENT
And many of the brethren in the Lord, waxing confident by my bonds are much more bold to speak the word without fear.
Philippians 1:14

From this day forward, walk in confidence believing that each day you are becoming the person you were meant to be. From this day forward, believe that everything you need is inside of you. From this day forward, believe that your latter years will be greater than your former years. From this day forward, believe that God has not brought you this far to leave you now. From this day forward, believe that your future will be much brighter than your past. From this day forward, believe that the very best is yet to come. From this day forward, believe that God has a blessing with your name on it. From this day forward, believe that you are more than a conqueror. From this day forward, believe that you are anointed and appointed for such a time as this. This is what I know for sure: There is more in my future than I have right now. Whatever the mind can conceive and believe, it can achieve!

CHAPTER 17
The Dress Looks Good on You

The blessing of the Lord maketh rich,
and he adds no sorrow with it.
Proverbs 10:22

Do you feel attractive? When you look in the mirror, what do you see? I am reminded of the line: "Mirror, Mirror on the wall who's the fairest of them all?" The question was posed each day by The Evil Queen in the story of "Snow White and the Seven Dwarfs." Every day she looked forward to her magic mirror telling her that she was by far the fairest of them all. Each day, The Evil Queen woke up and went to her mirror to receive her daily affirmation. However, one day the mirror revealed to her that Snow White was now the fairest of all in the land. The Evil Queen became outraged, and from that day forward she plotted Snow White's death. The power of a mirror.

Did you know that mirrors have been around for a very long time? Today, you can find a mirror almost everywhere. Mirrors have even become pieces of furniture in homes. A mirror gives us a true description, a detailed image, or a representation of our reflection. Most women look in the mirror at least once a day, and many say they don't like what they see. Most men don't look at all.

Most of the time, when I look in the mirror I am pleased with myself. Not because I am refreshed from a good night's sleep, but because I see myself as God sees me - a wonderful creation made in His own image.

"God sees us as a chosen generation, a royal priesthood, a holy nation, his own special people, that ye may proclaim the praises of him who called you out of the darkness into the marvelous light" (1 Peter 2:9). You are no longer walking in doom and gloom. You are no longer a silhouette. You are no longer a slave to your shadow. You are no longer a helpless baby bird in a nest. You were born to soar like an eagle, born to soar above the storms of life.

Do you feel beautiful? Do you feel comfortable in your own skin? Do you believe it when someone tells you that you are beautiful? Why not? Don't make excuses. Accept the compliment without hesitation or vacillation. Don't let another day go by without telling yourself that you are beautiful inside and out. Beauty is not so much in the eye of the beholder. Beauty is in your OWN eye. Beauty is *not* in your clothes, your hairstyle, your hips, your lips or fingertips. True beauty is developed from the inside out. It's an inside job.

Let me explain what I mean. For years, I compared myself to other women with "The If Game." If I looked like her. If I had longer hair. If I had better parents. If I were skinny. If I were rich. Personally, I had a laundry list of "ifs." Some are too embarrassing to list. I know I am not alone. I know you can feel me. Too many of us have put ourselves down – and far too many of us have let others put us down. Let's face it, we have settled for less than God's very best.

We must stop listening to the wrong voice. The wrong voice is negative self-talk. We inflict so much unnecessary suffering upon ourselves. It's mind boggling when you think about it. No wonder we have high blood pressure, migraine headaches, and suicidal thoughts. We must change our perception of who we are and the way others perceive us. We have entertained negative talk and negative feedback and it has restricted and immobilized us from moving forward. Here are four statements to avoid saying to yourself.

Number one: *I am not worthy.* This is a direct insult to your self-worth, self-image, and self-esteem. I have found out that many times we are our own worst enemies. What a man or woman thinks about themselves is what they become, whether it's good or bad. Speak words that build up your faith walk. Then, consistently make those words a lifestyle conviction. Keep in mind that you did not make yourself worthy. We were made worthy by what Jesus Christ did for us on the cross. His death, burial, and resurrection make every sinner and believer worthy.

Number two: *I don't deserve it.* This invalid statement about yourself is harmful and detrimental to your advancement in life. It's time to drain the swamp. One of the things that we must continue to work on is self-mastery. You must see yourself as having unlimited possibilities. You must see yourself beyond where you are right now. You can transform your existence no matter where you are in life. It starts by renewing the mind. The mind is very powerful, even more powerful than the body, because wherever the mind goes the body follows. What we think determines what we can or can't see or do. It was once said that, "The only difference between you and someone you envy is that you settled for less." That's powerful!

Number three: *I don't believe in myself.* Believing in yourself is the essential ingredient to achieving anything. I can't stress this enough. Believing in yourself is the key that opens the door to fulfillment. It has been said and proven that if you give proper time and energy to any activity, there is nothing that remains between you and your goals. If you are determined and steadfast, you can transform your life. My new mantra about the ABC's of life is: Put your faith into *action*. Believe what you say, and say what you *believe*. The new trend is *confidence*.

Number four: *I can't*. Saying you can't is debilitating. That phrase puts barricades between you and your goals. It implies failure before you even try. I took the word can't out of my dictionary. We all face difficult times in our lives. These difficult times can cause us to delay or quit. But, even if it's a very small step, it's important to dust yourself off and move forward. You can do it.

CHAPTER 18
Everyone is Unique

*Compare not yourself with anyone else
lest you spoil God's curriculum.*
Baal Shem Tov

I believe that everyone on the face of the Earth is unique. True beauty comes from feeling beautiful in your own skin. If we want to feel beautiful, we need to start by changing the way we think about beauty. Our culture says that beauty is an outward appearance, but Christ says that true beauty comes from the inside. Have you ever noticed a stranger from across the room at a restaurant, a fitness center, a holiday party or at a church gathering who was drop-dead gorgeous, but once you got to know Marilyn Magnificent or Steve Stunning a little better, suddenly he or she wasn't as attractive anymore? What about the reverse? Have you ever met someone who you thought was not so good looking, but once you spent some time with that person your impression changed for the better?

We see pictures of superstars and try to dress like them, perform like them; we even try to look like them (even though most of the pictures have been enhanced). We may even go as far as getting reconstructive surgery. But, instead of looking outside of the box, it would do us good to look within ourselves. When God created you, He made you one of a kind. You are unique in all of your ways. No one else has your exact set of fingerprints, not even your identical twin. Instead of idolizing supermodels on magazine covers, we should do a one eighty and start imitating the real supermodels, those who have modeled true beauty. They are all around us, they just don't crave attention by what they wear. You won't find them on the best runways or on the front page of a tabloid. You'll find them exemplifying Christ's love. The most beautiful women I know are those who focuses on making everyone around them feel beautiful by the small things they do for others. The way they live makes an impact.

True beauty is not fake ideology. True beauty is not lips, hips or fingertips. We live in a very simple-minded society. It is easy to condemn others by looking only at the surface. We see only the top layer of the skin – the epidermis. But, located under the epidermis, is the dermis –the thickest layer of your skin. In fact, the National Cancer Institute says that the dermis makes up 90% of the skin, in terms of overall thickness. Thin-minded people tend to look at the top layer of the skin – the epidermis; but, it's what's underneath the top layer that matters.

I shared this adage many chapters ago, but it bears repeating: "Don't Judge a Book by Its Cover." You cannot tell the quality of the book by the cover of the jacket or what holds its contents together. A book with a simple cover and title may be more relevant than a book with an extravagantly designed and titled cover. The prejudgment of a person, place or thing based solely on the outward appearance could cost you a meaningful friendship. Only by looking at the less obvious features can we know that the clothes on a person's back do not define who that person really is. How can we stop this "stinking thinking?" It starts by renewing the mind with positive thoughts and shedding the negative thoughts. Positive thoughts generate optimism. Negative thoughts generate pessimism. A positive and a negative cable might jump start your car battery, but their combination is useless when it comes to a positive mind-set. Look beyond the dress that she is wearing. Acknowledge that what you see on the outside is only a fraction of what's on the inside. Don't allow yourself to be labeled or limited by society's definition of your outward appearance. When it comes down to what's on the inside, your physical attributes and your clothing can never measure up to your compassion, kindness and empathy. I am not my dress. Real beauty is not in a dress. Real beauty is in the soul.

www.ingramcontent.com/pod-product-compliance
Lightning Source LLC
Chambersburg PA
CBHW072052290426
44110CB00014B/1656